Tricks for Trainers II

57 More Tricks and Teasers Guaranteed to Add Magic to Your Presentations!

Compiled by
Dave Arch

With an Introduction by:
Robert W. Pike, CSP

Published by

Resources for Organizations, Inc.

TRICKS FOR TRAINERS II

TABLE OF CONTENTS

(continued)

So why would we publish a second book of tricks for trainers?

There's an answer beyond the obvious—which is that the first book has been highly successful. This is the foundation concept of Creative Training Techniques® and magic can be a part of that. Magic captures the attention, fires up the imagination, and involves people. Have you ever said, "How did s/he do that?"

But the magic is the medium, the application and the learning point that comes along with it is the real message. And that's the real reason for this book—to give you the medium and let you supply the message or application.

For example, I use the magic coloring book in a number of seminars. The concept of the coloring book is simple: At first the pages are all blank, next they have outlines as any coloring book would have, then the outlines are fully colored, and finally the pages are all blank. The audience is astonished. The trick itself is fun, but it's the story that gives the application and that makes the point.

Let me illustrate. In Creative Training Techniques® I might close using the magic coloring book this way: designing and delivering a training program is a lot like a coloring book for your children or a niece or nephew. You want the coloring book to be personal, so you don't buy it, you make it. You take a colorful cover and staple it to a bunch of blank pages (Here you hold up the coloring book, show the cover, and riffle the pages to show the blank pages). Then you start to think about what subjects they would get excited about that would really pique their interest —it might be planes or trains, cowboys or astronauts, mountains, oceans, the zoo, or the circus. When you

decide on the topics you start tracing outlines on the blank pages (Riffle the pages to show the outlines). You do the same thing with a training program. You do a needs assessment to find out the skills and knowledge that would really pay off for the participants. You design the handouts, instructor materials, activities, and visual aids with that knowledge and those skills in mind. Yet at this point all we have is a training program—or a coloring book to color—neither means a thing until people are involved.

Now, there are three colors that computer monitors use to generate all the colors we see on a screen—red, green, and blue. I want you to get one of those colors in mind, imagine one of them in your fist, and when I count to three, yell out your choice and at the same time throw the imaginary color from your fist to the coloring book. (I hold the coloring book up.) If you yell loud enough we only do this once. (Generally there's laughter.) Ready, one...two...three. (Everybody yells their color and throws it at the book.) I then riffle the pages and they see all the color. Then I say, "You see it takes your energy, participation, and enthusiasm to make the coloring book really come to life. And you know without your energy, enthusiasm, and participation we have nothing at all." (I riffle the pages to show that they are blank again.) So, remember when it comes to training, you are the magic!

The story is important, because it is the story that helps apply the magic trick which they are involved in to some practical application—and the application is the key. In some cases in this book we supply you with an application. In other words, it's up to you. In future editions of this book we would like to supply applications that have worked for you with the various tricks. So write to me, tell me how you've used it, along with the story that you've used. And maybe, you'll see your story and name in the next edition!

How do I come up with stories? I start by practicing the trick without a story at all. My first goal is to master the steps so that I can perform the trick flawlessly without having to think about the steps. I also spend time practicing in front of the mirror or practicing with a video camera recording so that I can play it back and look at it from the audience's perspective. Along the way I start thinking about what each part of the trick might mean. I don't try to force it. I just think about it for a bit, then let my subconscious work on it. By the time I've mastered the trick, the story and application have taken shape.

Remember the story and application are as important as the trick. In training, we use magic to make a point—not simply to have fun, entertain, etc!

Some tricks you'll master quite easily—others will take more time, but it won't be long before you have half a dozen tricks you can use in various places. Here are a few other guidelines:

1.   Use the tricks sparingly and consider spacing them out. Don't let training get lost in the entertainment.

2.   Never perform a trick more than once. Most tricks are so simple that if the audience gets into a mode of trying to figure every one out they won't be listening to your story or application at all!

3.   Unless you are teaching an audience to do a trick, never reveal how it is done. The only reason for explaining how a trick is performed is to teach the person to perform it. No one appreciates having someone ruin a trick for an entire group by explaining it! Don't take away the wonder!

This book can be used in several ways:

1.   You can choose to go through it from cover to cover—to familiarize yourself with everything that's available. Then go back and learn the tricks you feel have application.

2.   You can start with tricks that you feel are easiest for you. That may be tricks with foolproof props like the magic coloring book, or the boomerangs, or tricks that require no props at all.

The most important thing to do, though, is to start somewhere. If at first a trick doesn't work the way you'd like, set it aside and come back to it a little later. All of the tricks in this book were designed to be as easy to master as possible for enthusiastic amateurs! So get ready to add a new dimension to your presentations—with *Tricks for Trainers*—magic with a message.

TRICKS FOR TRAINERS, VOL. II

Content Outline

Section One—TRICKS WITH SPECIAL PROPS
This section contains TEN different magic tricks.
Each magic trick is carefully selected to insure an adaptability to a
wide range of topics.

SPOTS BEFORE YOUR EYES!

This great card trick is ideal for emphasizing the role
of assumptions in leading us away from success. First
there is one spot on the card, then two, then three and
finally four! The application is easy and the card
opens to reveal a customized message written on a
reusable writing surface. A template is also included
with the book for making your own prop!

WHICH WAY DID IT GO?

This routine helps introduce a presentation involving
a search for key factors in any subject. The plaque is
designed with a reusable writing surface so that it can
be customized to the presentation. First the arrow
points one way and then another. . . finally the plaque
opens up to reveal the true focus of the presentation.
A template is included with the book for making your
own professional looking prop!

READ THE BOOK!

The trainer flips through a book appropriately titled
to the content. The class can see that the book contains a different word on each page. A person is asked
to select a page and concentrate on that word.
Suddenly, that word is the only word to be found on
any page. Each page in the book has that word on it!
Great for introducing a specific topic!

HOT STUFF!

The importance of mental attitude is underscored in this unbelievable demonstration. A small piece of tin foil is placed on each of the upturned palms of a volunteer. While the trainee concentrates on one piece of tin foil getting cold and one getting hot. . . suddenly, she screams and must drop the one piece of tin foil because it becomes too hot to handle! Nevertheless, when the piece is retrieved from the floor. . . it isn't hot at all! It must have all been in her mind!

THE MISSING PIECE!

A person from the training class is called to the overhead projector where a puzzle rests on the projection glass. Each person in the class will be able to watch this demonstration! Using the four pieces, the trainee is asked to assemble a giant dollar bill face down. No problem! It goes together easily! Now the pieces are turned face up and the trainee tries again. Now a piece is missing! How can it be? A piece is missing right out of the center of the bill! The trainer gives the person the missing piece from her pocket. The overhead shows that the missing piece contains a word describing the topic of the training! The missing piece has been found!

FRAMED!

An empty picture frame sits in the front of the class. The frame is covered with a cloth. Throughout the course of the class, the trainer keeps lifting the cloth to see if anything has appeared in the frame. Nothing happens. . . until the end of the class, when the cloth is removed and a summary statement has suddenly appeared under the glass! The class reads the statement in unison as a great finish to a training experience!

ELECTRONIC REVIEW BOARD

With a portable bulletin board and some parts from Radio Shack, you can build a reviewing tool that makes review more like playing a carnival game! Complete with light and buzzer, the group tries to find the button that will light the light and buzz the buzzer. The trainer can make it so that the group is either successful or not! Prizes and fun in review!

JUMBO FOUR CARD MONTE

Made from four large pieces of poster board, this magic trick works well when the trainer is speaking about the elimination of a factor in work performance (i.e. tardiness, uncooperativeness, etc.).

Three of the cards have positive qualities printed on them while one has a negative quality. The idea is to keep your eye on the negative quality. In spite of all good intentions, the negative quality disappears completely.

The handling of this routine is completely different from that published in the first volume of *Tricks For Trainers* since the face of each card is shown and consequently messages of several words can be utilized. The message can be any summarizing statement desired by the trainer to help cement the material in the minds of the learners!

SHORT CHANGED!

Using the large bills duplicated from the book, the trainer has one person play the part of the store cashier as the rest of the group experiences a lesson in being short changed. Try as they will, the group has great difficulty figuring just when the short change

takes place! It's a great energizer as the group comes to understand how easily the mind can be manipulated!

COINCIDENTALLY!

This trick uses ten large cards made from pieces of poster board capable of carrying any message desired by the trainer.

A volunteer is brought to the front of the room and given five cards—being told to put the cards behind his back. The trainer does likewise with his five cards.

Each removes one card from the cards behind his back without looking and hands it to the other person. Each now takes the card he has just been handed and reverses it as he puts it among the cards remaining in his hand.

When the cards are brought out from behind the backs, it is found that both persons chose the exact same card from his five. In fact all of the other cards carry messages exactly the opposite of the two chosen cards. If the word EXCELLENCE was written on the two cards and MEDIOCRE written on all the others, the following transition into the material could easily be used. . .
"Today in this session. . . we will be attempting to locate and identify EXCELLENCE when we see it. We will attempt to lift it above work we would only call MEDIOCRE!"

Section Two—PROPLESS MAGIC FOR TRAINERS

These TEN tricks require items that are not prepared and can quite often be borrowed from members of the training group.

SCISSORS RACE

A contest is held between two members of the training class for a truly great prize. The prize could even be a new car! Each is given an adding machine paper strip scotch taped into a long circular ring. The goal is to cut around the ring separating the initial ring into two separate rings. The first one to do just that without tearing their paper wins the car! The trainer first demonstrates and then begins the race. However, at the end of the race one person ends up with two rings linked together and the other finishes with one giant ring! No one wins the prize, but everyone learns a little bit more about examining the situation before jumping in!

HATS. . . HATS . . .HATS!

Using a single piece of newspaper, the trainer tells a story of a small boy who would play for days with just such a piece of paper. The paper is folded into a series of hats, a ship, and finally a shirt as the story unfolds. It's an inspiring story whose creativity always intrigues a training group!

THE TISSUE TRICK

The trainer claims that she has just learned a new magic trick that uses a tissue. Slowly she tears the tissue and clumsily switches the pieces for another tissue—claiming to have restored the tissue. However during the trick, the group can't help but

notice that during the switch the actual pieces have now fallen from her hand to the floor. Not to worry!

She picks up the fallen pieces and restores them too! An added bonus idea is given using a piece of colored tissue paper with customized content printed on the paper!

BUSTED!

Again the trainer claims to have mastered a magic trick using a large empty grocery sack and a balloon that completely fills the inside of the sack. The inflated balloon is placed into the sack. The trainer will now attempt to run a long needle through the outside of the sack through the balloon and out the other side of the sack without hurting the balloon at all! Slowly the needle is inserted. Suddenly, a loud noise signifies that the balloon has broken! Oh well, the trainer exclaims, "I always carry a spare!" Another completely inflated balloon is now removed from inside the sack!

With a magic marker, words can be printed on the balloons to enhance content delivery!

MONEY TO WEAR

Great for use when emphasizing cost control or for building a sense of being #1 in an industry! Each person is given a one dollar bill to wear on their finger! That's right! The bill is folded into a perfectly shaped ring with the number ONE right on top in the signet position! They look great and helps to bring a group together. The dollar bill is only folded. It is not torn or mutilated in any way!

DOUBLE EXPOSURE

Imagine taking a Polaroid picture of your training group only to have a summary word or statement mysteriously appear in the picture—floating above their heads! They'll talk about this one for a long time!

FLASH!

Holding a flashcube in her otherwise empty hand, the trainer moves around the room with this "portable volunteer finder." Suddenly, as she approaches one of the trainees, there is a bright flash as one of the bulbs ignite. This process can be repeated with all four of the bulbs in the flashcube if desired. Or use it as an energizer with the group holding hands and rubbing their feet on the floor until the static electricity causes the bulb to ignite! Great fun!

STEP RIGHT UP I!

Don't just point to someone when you need a volunteer. Select them by magic! Four large cards (patterns supplied in the book) are used with words printed on each card. When the cards are selected and then read in order, they say "LET'S HAVE SOMEONE VOLUNTEER. . . THAT'S A GOOD IDEA! . . . WHO WILL DO IT? . . . I WILL!" Even though the selection looks random, the trainer actually has complete control over who gets the final "I will" card. A great joke to pull on that fun-loving person in the training group.

STEP RIGHT UP II!

After you've used "Step Right Up I," use this one by adding two more cards to the four used before! The same person still gets the volunteer card! He'll know he's being picked on now!

DIVIDE AND DECIDE!

This is an apparently random way of giving away a prize to one of the trainees. Even though there are six very expensive prizes and one inexpensive prize, the trainee always gets the inexpensive prize!

Section Three—TEACH THEM A TRICK

The following magic tricks are designed to be performed and then taught to the members of the training class to help emphasize a point with hands-on involvement.

INVISIBLE BALL TRICK

With a paper lunch sack and their imaginations, the trainees will be doing "invisible ball juggling" in no time! With a little musical background, it's great fun as they actually hear the balls land in their sacks!

RAINBOW WHEEL

This black and white wheel can be made into a top by inserting a short pencil through the center hole. Then when it's spun on the tabletop, colors appear in the wheel. It's great for illustrating how we can often see the positive in situations if we just look closely enough!

CHALLENGE VANISH

The trainer places any content oriented item under a handkerchief. Group members feel the item under the handkerchief. Suddenly, the trainer whips the handkerchief away and the item is gone! The handkerchief may be examined! When this one is explained to the group, many applications present themselves.

OVERHEAD!

One of the trainees leaves the room so he cannot see what's happening in the room but remains within listening distance. The trainer moves around the room holding her hand above different members' heads and saying simply the word "overhead." Then she stops

and says "Over whose head?" and the out-of-the-room trainee correctly names the person where the trainer has stopped. This is repeated until someone in the group begins to figure out how it's done! This one really requires great observational skills!

A LITTLE HELP FROM MY FRIENDS

This time several trainees are led from the room and brought back in one by one as the trainer presents a magic trick with the help of others in the group. Eventually, the trainees begin to catch on to how the magic is done and the importance of observation is underscored again!

GENIUS TEST

Made from a playing card, a string and two washers, this puzzle challenges the most creative as they seek to remove the washers without damaging the card! Great for encouraging creative problem solving!

COUNTING SHEEP

No matter how slowly the trainer states the question, the group has trouble understanding what he's trying to say. Great for working on communication and listening skills!

WIN! WIN!

Using an old carnival game, the trainer illustrates the nature of a win-win negotiation!

PSYCHIC CONTENT REVIEW

This mindreading trick can be customized to any content review (thirty questions). As the trainees work the trick on each other, they are actually reviewing the material!!!

FOLLOW THE LEADER

The directions are given slowly by the trainer and even demonstrated. Nevertheless, the group finds it very difficult to successfully complete the action. This works excellently for demonstrating the importance of detailing our communications.

LIAR! LIAR!

With a television gameshow format, the trainer successfully tells time and time again which of two people is lying in response to his question. The group really interacts as they seek to find the solution to this fun exercise!

IT'S GONE!

Working with a small puzzle of three pieces, the trainees receive a graphic illustration of the vanishing (or appearing) of a key piece of content. Even though they hold the pieces in their hands and do the magic themselves, this one is not easily explained!

Section Four—EARLY BIRD FUN

This section contains SIX audience tested early bird exercises that involve the audience in the material before the seminar even begins!

EXERCISE #1

This maze can be customized to content. Comes complete with handout and transparency masters. Can your trainees find their way from the beginning to the end of this challenging maze?

EXERCISE #2

This classic puzzle comes with three pieces. Can your trainees arrange the three pieces so that the two jockeys are riding on top of the two horses? Complete with handout and transparency masters.

EXERCISE #3

Arranging these pieces into a cross isn't as easy as it first seems! Complete with handout and transparency masters.

EXERCISE #4

This puzzle looks like it would take geometry, calculus, or trigonometry to solve! Yet, it's more simple than that as soon as your trainees sift through the unnecessary details. Transparency master included.

EXERCISE #5

Can your class figure out how to cut a hole in an index card big enough for a full-size person to walk through it? They will be able to once you show them how! Most amazing!

EXERCISE #6

Using this ancient-appearing board containing jumbles of letters, group members can follow the instructions and find up to five different messages hidden in the board. These messages may be content oriented. It seems so mysterious when the messages begin to appear!

Section Five—BRAINTWISTERS

This section contains EIGHT different braintwisters. When presented by the trainer in a challenging manner it always makes an audience think creatively and sets the mood for a great time of interaction.

BRAINTWISTER #1

A picture of a table is placed on the overhead. What is the largest American coin that can be placed on the tabletop without touching any of its sides? The answer will surprise everyone!

BRAINTWISTER #2

A transparency with a picture of an old lady is placed on the overhead. By turning it upside down, the lady changes into a young girl. It's all a matter of perspective!

BRAINTWISTER #3

Without moving this picture on the overhead, the class sees the picture from four different perspectives. The picture literally moves itself in their minds! A great illustration of differing viewpoints!

BRAINTWISTER #4

A picture of a Baker is on the overhead. Can anyone find the cow in the picture? As the picture is turned upside down, the obvious picture of a cow comes into view.

BRAINTWISTER #5

A picture of a gold brick is cut into several pieces and reassembled only to find that it's grown one entire cubic inch! How can this work with the pieces remaining the same size!

BRAINTWISTER #6

How many times will you need to wrap a string around your head in order to equal your height.
The answer will surprise you, and you'll have fun proving it too!

BRAINTWISTER #7

Can you remove the mug from the string hanging around your neck? It's not as easy as it sounds!

BRAINTWISTER #8

Can you remove the scissors from the string hanging around your neck? It's harder than the mug!

Section Six—**BONUS SECTION**

This bonus section contains NINE quick ideas that add
fun and excitement to training sessions by
capitalizing on the unexpected!

PHONE NUMBER READING

At anytime during the training convince the rest of the
group that you can tell anyone their phone number
without ever having met them!

PHONE BOOK THROW

When you toss this phone book to someone in the
back row, everyone ducks! Then they laugh! Great
fun! Things are not always what they first appear!

THE SHIRT OFF MY BACK

Imagine grabbing someone's shirt by the collar and
pulling it off even though they are still wearing their
coat! You can!

UNRAVELED

When one of your trainees is nice enough to pick at a
thread on your coat, it suddenly pulls away and
becomes over twenty feet in length!

PRIZES! PRIZES! PRIZES!

These five prizes are perfect to use in a training situation! They sound so impressive. . . but are really so inexpensive!

A FINAL TRICK
WITH TRICKS 4 TRAINERS, VOL. II

Use this book to make magic!

TRICKS FOR TRAINERS II

SECTION ONE

Tricks With Special Props

This section contains TEN different magic tricks.
Each magic trick is carefully selected to ensure an
adaptability to a wide range of topics.

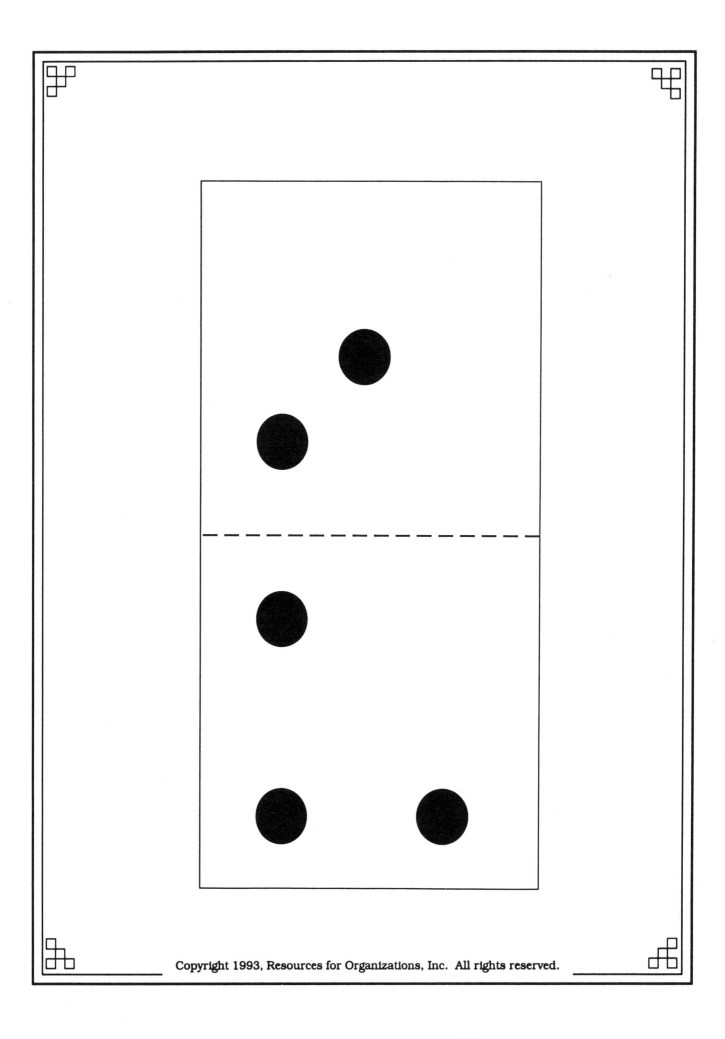

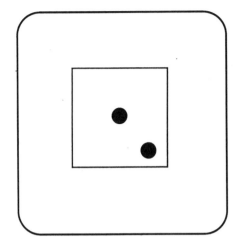

Side A

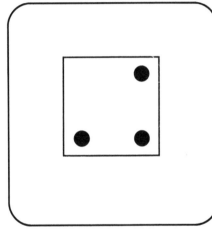

Side B

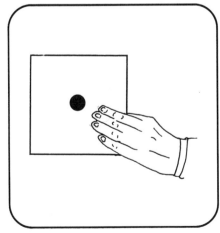

figure 1

SPOTS BEFORE YOUR EYES!

This great card trick is ideal for emphasizing the role of assumptions in leading us away from success. First there is one spot on the card, then two, then three and finally four! The application is easy and the card opens to reveal a customized message written on a reusable writing surface. A template is also included with the book for making your own prop!

When you desire to show just how ingrained our assumptions can become, there is no better demonstration!

Duplicate onto heavy card stock the master you see on the preceding page. Cut it out around the dark lines folding it in half at the dotted line.

One side of the card should now have two spots on it *(SIDE A)* with the other side having three spots in the corners *(SIDE B)*.

The instructions that follow always use the terms "left" and "right" to refer to the trainer's perspective of left and right.

Pick up the card so that your left hand holds the card with Side A facing the audience. The hand is holding the card by the lower left-hand corner with its fingers extending to cover the spot in the lower left-hand corner of Side A *(figure 1)*. The audience should not be aware of this extra spot. It should look to the audience as though they are looking at a dice with one spot facing them. Say the word "ONE" to help reinforce this assumption.

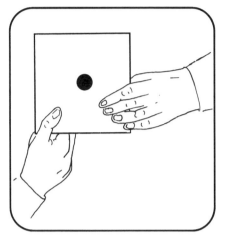

Figure 2

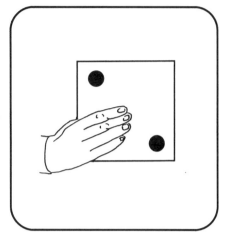

Figure 3

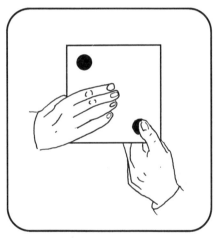

Figure 4

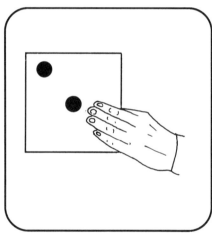

Figure 5

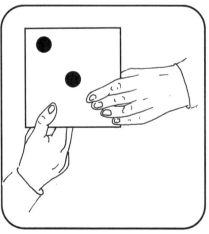

Figure 6

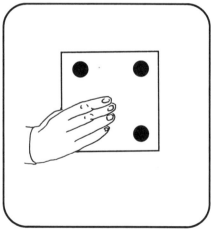

Figure 7

Bring your right hand into play palm towards the audience and grasp the card in the lower right-hand corner with your fingers extended to cover the spot in that corner on Side B *(figure 2)*. Turn the card over so that your right hand continues to hold the card by the lower right-hand corner.

The audience will now be looking at Side B of the card. It should look as though they are seeing the side of the dice with two spots showing (in opposite corners). Say the word "TWO" to help reinforce this assumption *(figure 3)*.

Bring your left hand up with its palm towards the audience and grasp the card in the lower left-hand corner using your extended fingers to cover the blank spot in that corner on Side A *(figure 4)*.

Turn the card over so that your left hand continues to hold the card by the lower left-hand corner. The audience is now looking at Side A and it should look as though they are seeing the THREE side of the dice with one spot simply covered by your fingers *(figure 5)*. Say the word "THREE" to reinforce the audience's assumption.

Finally, bring your right hand palm towards the audience and grasp the card in the lower right-hand corner with your extended fingers covering the blank spot in that corner Side B *(figure 6)*.

Turn the card over so that your right hand continues to hold the card by that lower right-hand corner *(figure 7)*. The audience is now looking at Side B. It should look as though they are seeing

the FOUR side of the dice with one of the corner spots covered by your fingers. Say "FOUR!"

You are now ready to begin the sequence all over again showing the four sides of this two sided card.

When you are done showing the mysteries of this card, you can then open the card up like a book and have any message you desire printed inside to give a strong finish to this demonstration!

THE STRONGEST USE OF THIS CARD has been in the possible applications as you teach the group how to do the routine. You can duplicate enough of the cards so that each person in your training group has one.

As they see the role assumptions play in being fooled, they will better appreciate how limiting assumptions can be!

30   Tricks for Trainers II

WHICH WAY DID IT GO?

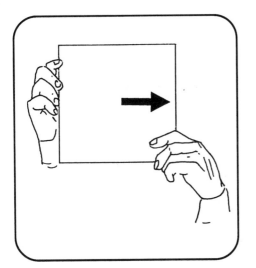

figure 1

This routine helps introduce a presentation involving a search for key factors in any subject. The plaque is designed with a reusable writing surface so that it can be customized to the presentation. First the arrow points one way and then another. . . finally the plaque opens up to reveal the true focus of the presentation. A template is included with the book for making your own professional looking prop!

Duplicate the master on the next page onto heavy card stock. Cut it out around the dark lines and then fold it in half at the dotted line.

You should then have a card with an arrow on each side of the card. The arrows point at right angles to each other.

The following directions always use the terms "left" and "right" to refer to the trainer's perspective.

Begin by holding the card with your right hand in the lower right-hand corner and your left hand in the upper left-hand corner. The arrow on your side of the card should be pointing straight up with the arrow on the audience side of the card pointing to YOUR left *(figure 1)*. This is always the starting position. You need to be very familiar with it.

Turn the card over with your fingers giving the card a spin. Keep your right hand in the lower right-hand corner and your left hand in the upper left-hand corner. As you spin the card

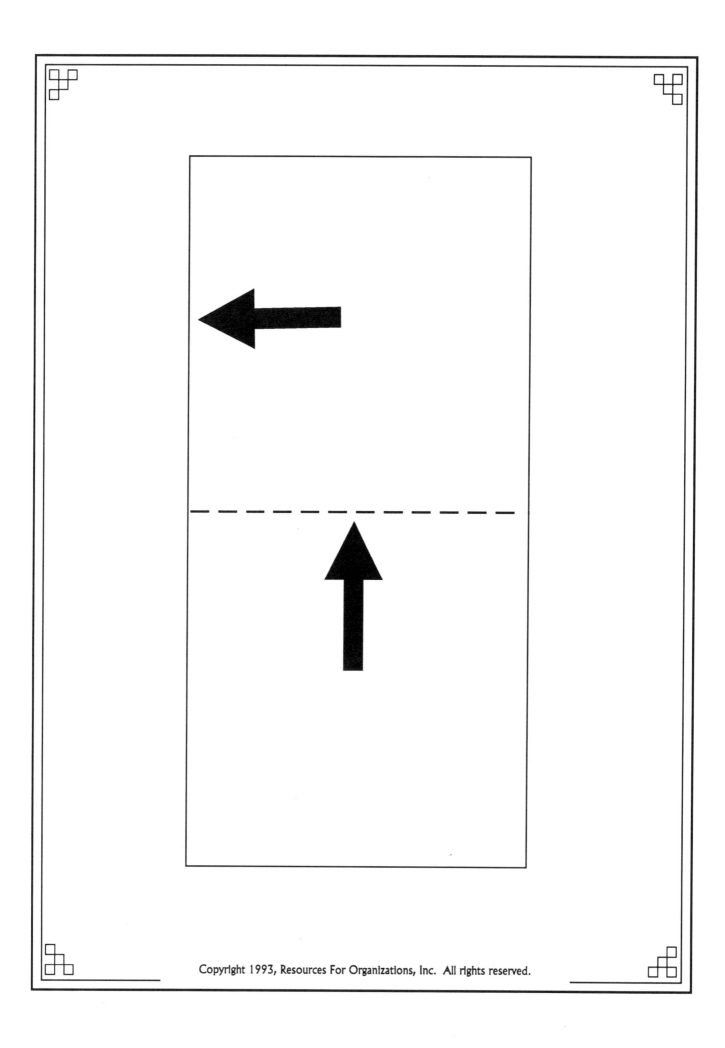

several times, it will appear to the audience that you have a two sided card with arrows on both sides pointing the same direction.

Now move your right hand up to the upper right-hand corner and your left hand down to the lower left-hand corner and spin the card again. Now as you spin the card, it will appear to the audience that you have a two sided card with arrows on both sides pointing in the opposite directions!

If you stop spinning the card when the arrow on your side of the card is pointing up, you can turn the card over END FOR END and show the audience that the arrow on the other side really points up!

If you stop spinning the card when the arrow on your side of the card is pointing down, you can turn the card over END FOR END and show the audience that the arrow on the other side of the card really points down!

A suggested presentation follows. . .

"As you can see my arrow has SUCCESS printed on it. I'm not sure how each of us might define success (spin the card showing arrows pointing in the same direction). For some people it might be income. If they achieve a certain salary level, then they feel successful (spin the card so that the arrows point in opposite directions).

(Suddenly realize that something is wrong and straighten out the arrows. . . spinning the card

so that both arrows point in the same direction again.)

Others might consider family and friends more important. When the family is getting along or they have friends around them that like them, that's when they feel most successful.

(As before, spin the card with arrows facing the same direction. Then shift your hands while talking and spin the card so that suddenly the arrows are confused again.)

(Suddenly realize that something is wrong and straighten out the arrows. . . spinning the card so that both arrows point in the same direction again.)

Possibly you would define "SUCCESS" with something completely different!

(Stop spinning the card and turn the card over END FOR END showing that the arrow is now point UP!)

Whatever your personal definition, we will be exploring today the role of

_____!

(At this point, you can open the card to reveal the message that will introduce your topic!)

READ THE BOOK!

The trainer flips through a book appropriately titled to the content. The class can see that the book contains a different word on each page. A person is asked to select a page and concentrate on that word. Suddenly, that word is the only word to be found on any page. Each page in the book has that word on it! Great for introducing a specific topic!

Design a book comprised of about fifty 8 ½" x 11" pages. Twenty-five of those pages should be trimmed ⅛" shorter so that they are approximately 8 ⅜" x 11". Now assemble the book with the shorter pages being every other page in the book. A longer page should start the book. Bind it with the fanciest binding system you can access. How you proceed from this point will depend upon your application. We will use an example.

If you wanted to introduce the topic of communication in creating a successful office environment, you might title the book KEYS TO A SUCCESSFUL WORKPLACE—giving it a nice cover label.

On each of the longer pages you would print a different component that makes for a successful workplace (i.e. mutual respect, quality work, etc.). On each of the shorter pages, you would only print the same word—COMMUNICATION.

Print the words so that the word is printed lengthwise on the page with the top of the word closest to the binding. Print the words as large as possible with a pen that doesn't show through the paper to the other side. You will now notice something unusual about your book. When you

flip the pages from the front to the back, you will see different words. In other words, only the longer pages will show. However, when you flip from the back to the front of the book only the word COMMUNICATION will show.

When you're ready to use the book, display it to the group showing the title to this great work. Flip through the book from the front to the back stopping every so often to show the multitude of different ingredients needed to create a successful workplace. Select a volunteer to choose one of the topics. Turn your head away and flip through the book (from back to front) asking your volunteer to stop you whenever they desire.

When they say "Stop," stop at that point and open the book to show them and the class the word they selected. Of course, it will be the word COMMUNICATION. Close the book and toss it down on a table.

Ask the person to concentrate on the selected word and you will attempt to pick up the word mentally. Slowly and dramatically begin to get the word letter by letter to the amazement of the group. Offer to show the group how it's done (however, as you'll see, you never really do explain the entire working). Pick up the book again and flip through the book for the group from back to front to show the group that there really is only one word in the book —COMMUNI-CATION! Your volunteer only had one choice! Communication is the true key to a great office.

You've captured their attention through involvement, and they're ready to hear what you have to say!

HOT STUFF!

This trick involves heat and a poisonous substance.
Extreme care needs to be taken.
Be careful to follow the directions exactly for safety.
Do not use with children.

The importance of mental attitude is underscored in this unbelievable demonstration. A small piece of tin foil is placed on each of the upturned palms of a volunteer. While the trainee concentrates on one piece of tin foil getting cold and one getting hot. . . suddenly, she screams and must drop the one piece of tin foil because it becomes too hot to handle! Nevertheless, when the piece is retrieved from the floor. . . it isn't hot at all! It must have all been in her mind!

This most unusual demonstration uses the little known property of a chemical that can be ordered by any drug store. Simply ask for Mercury Bichloride Tablets.

SINCE IT IS POISONOUS, PLEASE HANDLE IT WITH RESPECT.

Crush and dissolve one tablet into a small pill vial of water. Obtain a small metal tin box (like a Sucrets box) and cut a sponge to fit inside the box. Before performing, soak the sponge with the liquid placing that box in your briefcase with the lid open so that you can moisten your index and thumb of one hand as you reach for the tin foil in your briefcase with the other hand.

The properties of this chemical on tin foil are quite remarkable. When transferred from your moistened fingers to the tin foil, you will be able to tear off a piece of tin foil—rolling it into a ball without the ball becoming hot as long as you hold it pinched between your fingers. However, when you place the small tin foil ball on the

outstretched palm of a volunteer (and it makes contact with the air), it will become hot within a matter of seconds. It will become so hot that the spectator will need to drop it.

WARNING: ALWAYS HAVE THE VOLUN-TEER'S HAND COMPLETELY EXTENDED! NEVER HAVE THEM CLOSE THEIR HAND AROUND THE BALL! THEY MUST BE ABLE TO DROP THE BALL IMMEDIATELY!

In performance, talk about mental attitude and the power of the mind over what we see and experience. Offer to demonstrate as you select a volunteer. Reach into your briefcase and remove a piece of tin foil while moistening your thumb and index finger on the sponge. Take the piece of tin foil between your moistened fingers and then tear off a piece of the tin foil with your non-moistened hand. Roll it into a small ball (about pea size) and place it on the outstretched palm of one of the volunteer's hands. Have her concentrate on that ball getting cold.

Taking the larger piece of tin foil back into your non-moistened fingers, use your moistened fingers to tear off a piece of the tin foil—rolling it also into a small ball. Tell the volunteer to concentrate on this ball becoming hot. Place the ball on her other outstretched hand.

She will in all probability shriek within seconds and drop the hot ball to the ground. If you pick up the ball now from the ground. . . you will find that it's not even warm! Interview her briefly asking what happened, thank her and have her return to her seat.

THE MISSING PIECE!

A person from the training class is called to the overhead projector where a puzzle rests on the projection glass.

Each person in the class will be able to watch this demonstration! Using the four pieces, the trainee is asked to assemble a giant dollar bill face down. No problem! It goes together easily!

Now the pieces are turned face up and the trainee tries again. Now a piece is missing! How can it be? A piece is missing right out of the center of the bill! The trainer gives the person the missing piece from her pocket. The overhead shows that the missing piece contains a word describing the topic of the training! The missing piece has been found!

This is a most unusual illustration because even when you experience this you probably won't be able to explain exactly why it works!

CAREFULLY use the pattern supplied with this book to cut the puzzle pieces from (two), one dollar bills. One bill will make the face up pieces and one the face down pieces. Use a utility knife and a ruler to make sure your cuts are accurate to the pattern. The angles of cutting are very important to the successful working of this great illusion. Then take the pieces and after aligning them carefully, use a glue stick to glue the same numbered pieces back-to-back.

Now continue this process with each piece—gluing each piece back-to-back to its other matching number piece.

Tricks for Trainers II   **39**

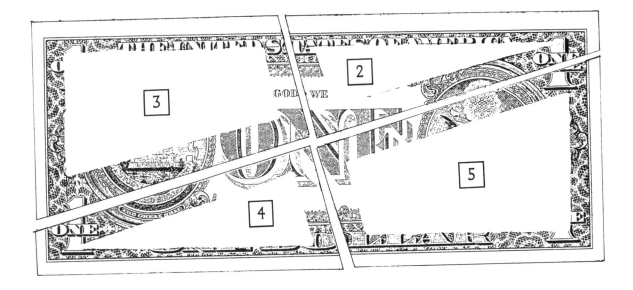

After completing the gluing process, take the pieces and attempt to build the dollar bill face down. You will find that it goes together perfectly with only FOUR pieces!

Now turn the pieces face up and build the bill. You'll find that you will need George Washington's face in order to make a complete bill!

To use this in a training session, cut a piece of transparency material the same size as the "George Washington's face piece." On that piece, carefully print a key word that summarizes your training (i.e. QUALITY, SERVICE, etc.). You will use this transparency piece for the final missing piece. Keep that piece out of sight.

Invite a volunteer to come up to the overhead and show the group the four puzzle pieces (without "the George Washington's face piece)." Place them face down on the overhead projection glass. Have the volunteer attempt to assemble the bill. No problem!

Now turn the pieces over (mixing them up as you do) and invite the volunteer to assemble the bill face up. There will be a surprised expression as they discover that one piece is missing—right out of the middle!

Suddenly realize that you have the missing piece and drop the transparency piece into the middle! The word will show on the overhead—giving you a natural lead in to your material!

FRAMED!

An empty picture frame sits in the front of the class. The frame is covered with a cloth. Throughout the course of the class, the trainer keeps lifting the cloth to see if anything has appeared in the frame. Nothing happens. . . until the end of the class, when the cloth is removed and a summary statement has suddenly appeared under the glass! The class reads the statement in unison as a great finish to a training experience!

Select a regular picture frame (8 x 10 or larger) that contains a glass front, with a backing piece held in place by clips around the frame.

You will also need an opaque black cloth with which to cover the frame.

Design any summarizing statement you desire and have it printed on a card so that it fills the frame.

However, before you put the printed card in the frame, cut another piece of black material (satin works great). This piece should be the same size as the frame's backing piece of cardboard plus about an inch and a half extra on the top edge of the frame.

When assembling the frame for your presentation, place your printed card face up on top of the backing piece of cardboard and place your black piece of material on top of the printed card—inserting all of this into the frame with the

extra inch and a half of material from the black
material hanging behind the frame away from the
audience's view.

The frame should now look empty. Iron the piece
of black covering material if wrinkles show
through the glass.

Cover the entire frame with the larger opaque
cloth—checking throughout the presentation for
anything appearing in the frame.

Finally, when ready to reveal the message, grip
the hidden flap of material through the covering
cloth and pull both off together. Since you pulled
the black piece of material away from in front of
your summary statement, it will suddenly have
appeared in the frame!

Have your training class read it in unison to help
reinforce your central message!

ELECTRONIC REVIEW BOARD

With a portable bulletin board and some parts from Radio Shack, you can build a reviewing tool that makes review more like playing a carnival game! Complete with light and buzzer, the group tries to find the button that will light the light and buzz the buzzer. The trainer can make it so that the group is either successful or not! Prizes and fun in review!

Your audience must believe that this review board is a high-tech product with an intricate internal computer system that randomly changes which of five buttons lights the light on the board.

You must never lose sight of this perspective as you build and operate the board.

In order to build the board, you will need:

1 Small portable bulletin board
5 Small push button switches (#275-617)
1 Battery holder for 4 AA batteries (#270-391A)
1 Buzzer (Archer 6V/#273-054)
1 Bulb Base (#272-325)
1 Bulb (#272-1123)
1 Set of peel and stick vinyl numbers
1 Roll of bell wire (#278-1224)
1 Soldering Gun and Solder

At the time of this writing all of the above will cost less than $20 plus the cost of the bulletin board!

WIRING DIAGRAM

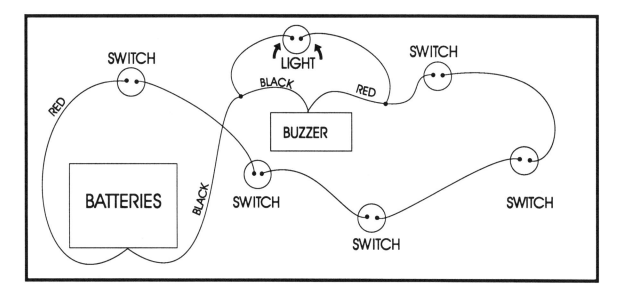

BACK OF BULLETIN BOARD

Layout your bulletin board arranging the push buttons in a pattern to suit your style of teaching. The diagram has the buttons randomly placed on the bulletin board with the light in the middle at the top of the board.

Make holes in your bulletin board and insert all of the switches and the lightbulb in your selected locations. Take your vinyl numbers and number your switches 1-5.

Now, on the back of the board, use either silicone or double faced carpet tape to attach the battery pack and the buzzer as shown in the diagram.

You are now ready to wire the back of the board. Follow the diagram carefully and all will be well. Insert the batteries in the holder and your Review Board is ready to go.

Although we will suggest several different ideas for using the board, it is necessary for you to know the following basics before we begin.

INITIAL PREPARATION

Before beginning the review game, you must set the board for operation. To set the board follow the pattern below—pushing each of the buttons in the following order:

1. . . 2. . . 3. . . 4. . . 5. . .4 . . .3 . . 2. . . 1

When moving through that sequence of numbers, STOP pushing the buttons as soon as the light lights. Push that button off and then push each

of the other buttons once. You're now ready to
start!

IF USING LESS THAN FIVE REVIEW POINTS
(with your electronic review board). . . set the
board per the instructions above but once the
light lights, DON'T push the buttons you won't be
using! Only push the buttons you will be using in
the review game!

THE PROCESS FOR LETTING A PERSON WIN

When you want someone to win, have the person
pick a number. Push one of the other buttons
showing him that it doesn't light the light. Give
him an opportunity to change his mind about the
number he selected. Push another number he
DOESN'T choose and give him an opportunity to
change his mind again. In other words, be sure
and push all of the other buttons first—pushing
his chosen button last! Remember that once the
game is set (see Initial Preparation section) the
last button pushed will always light the light.

Again reset the machine by pushing off the
button that lights the light and then pushing each
of the other buttons once.

HERE IS THE PROCESS FOR MAKING A PERSON LOSE

Have the person choose a number and push the
button. . . the light will not light. Show him now
that other buttons also do not light the light but
one does. Remember, the last button you push
always lights the light. As you push the other
wrong buttons, act as though even you aren't
sure which one will light the light this time.

Again reset the machine by pushing off the button that lights the light and then pushing each of the other buttons once.

SUGGESTED REVIEW ROUTINE

Have your main points printed on cards thumb-tacked to the board with one by each button. On one side of the card have the information in the form of a question and on the backside have the information stated in the form of an answer to that question (i.e. What is a training technique in which people play different parts in a scenario? (ROLE PLAY).

During a break, quietly explain to one of the trainees that you are doing some magic in the next session and would really like to borrow their watch as part of a trick. Thank them for their watch and place it in your pocket until ready to do the review.

As soon as you're ready to review, have the cards removed from the bulletin board shuffled and then tacked back up randomly by different numbers with the question side of each card facing the group. Remove the watch from your pocket and in your best barker voice let the class know that now comes the time in the class when they will get a chance to win a lovely watch!

Go into a description of the watch—never looking at the individual whose watch it is. People will want to play the game! If the person indicates that it's their watch, simply make some comment to the rest of the group like "They're quite confident aren't they? Well, we'll sure let

them play if they want to."

Point to someone in the group and ask them to pick one number on the board. Don't have them press it yet.

Then have another person select a question and a corresponding numbered button.

Continue this way until all of the buttons except one have been selected and then turn to the person whose watch it is and have her select a button (of course, it's not much of a choice since only one button remains).

Have each person first answer their question and then press their selection—making sure that the person whose watch it is does go last. After the first one has pushed the button, give the second spectator a chance to change buttons with the spectator who owns the watch.

Finally, the class member wins the watch back! Congratulate her on a job well done and compliment her on the beauty of the watch!

The great fun of this routine lies in the fact that the spectator has watched others get excited about the watch not knowing that it is her watch. Content has been covered by the class and visually reinforced through the signage.

And you have received all of the excitement from an expensive giveaway without breaking your training budget. Hopefully, the company will share the extra savings with you in your next raise!

JUMBO FOUR CARD MONTE

Made from four large pieces of poster board, this magic trick works well when the trainer is speaking about the elimination of a factor in work performance (i.e. tardiness, uncooperativeness, etc.).

Three of the cards have positive qualities printed on them while one has a negative quality. The idea is to keep your eye on the negative quality. In spite of all good intentions, the negative quality disappears completely.

The handling of this routine is completely different from that published in the first volume of *Tricks For Trainers* since the face of each card is shown and consequently messages of several words can be utilized.

The message can be any summarizing statement desired by the trainer to help cement the material in the minds of the learners!

The cards you make should be made from card stock approximately 5" x 7" in size.

You will need to make ONE card with a negative quality printed on it and FOUR cards with the same positive quality printed on each one.

Carefully glue one of the positive quality cards to the backside of the negative quality card. You are now ready to begin the routine.

If you find that this back-to-back card is conspicuously thick, go ahead and glue blank cards to the back of the other cards so that they all become uniformly thick.

In the following directions, the four cards you have made will be referred to by the following letters:

Card A/B is actually two cards glued back to back.
Side A is the positive quality card.
Side B matches the other cards.

Card C is the match for side B of Card A/B.

Card D is a match for Cards B, C, and E.

Card E is a match for Cards B, C, and D.

When you get ready to perform this magic trick, the cards need to be in following order from front to back with the faces of the cards facing your audience:

Card A/B with side A facing the audience.

Card C behind Card A/B with its face towards the audience.

Card D behind Card C with its face towards the audience.

Card E behind Card D with its face towards the audience.

Put the cards in that order into a manilla envelope and you are ready to present it anytime during the training session.

Note: This trick cannot be performed with anyone sitting directly behind you.

In performing this great magic trick, fan the cards in the above order so that your audience can see all of the faces.

Explain to them that this is an old game that people have used to take money from unsuspecting victims. The people who played the game needed to keep track of the card (point to the A side of Card A/B to indicate the odd card).

Close the fan and pretend to turn over Card A/B. Actually what you will do is to turn over both Card A/B and Card C together so that the back of Card C will face the audience. Explain to the audience that the operator of this game always turned the odd card away from his audience to begin the game.

THIS IS THE ONLY SECRET MOVE IN THE ENTIRE MAGIC TRICK SO BE SURE YOU PRACTICE IT SO THAT YOU CAN TURN THE TWO CARDS OVER JUST AS THOUGH THEY WERE ONE CARD.

Fan the cards and you will see that only one card now has its back to the audience. People will assume that it's the negative quality card. You know better!

"Let's make it easy on you the first time," you say as you remove Card A/B from the fan putting it down on the table.

Be careful to not show the back of Card A/B while putting it down onto the table!

Show your fan again in which one card still has its back to the audience. Turn another card so that its back is also towards the audience. This will confuse them even more. Mix the cards and ask the audience which card they believe to be the negative quality card.

Whichever one they pick, show them that it's NOT and put the card they chose on the table. You still have one card of the two cards left with its back towards the audience. Turn the other card around too and mix the cards.

Ask them again which card they believe now is the odd colored card. Show them that again they would have lost money and put that card on the table.

Now. . . pretend to mix up in your hand the only card still left. Smile as you ask the audience which card they believe now is the negative quality card. Explain that at this point in the game most people would bet all of their money on this one single card. Of course. . . again for the third time show the audience that they would have lost money!

The odd card was always completely gone by this time in the game!

"That's exactly what we're going to attempt to do in this training session. We will be looking for the negative qualities that hinder our performance— learning how to make them disappear!"

SHORT CHANGED!

Using the large bills duplicated from the book, the trainer has one person play the part of the store cashier as the rest of the group experiences a lesson in being short changed. Try as they will, the group has great difficulty figuring just when the short change takes place! It's a great energizer as the group comes to understand how easily the mind can be manipulated!

Copy the large bills supplied with this routine so that you have five one dollar bills, one five dollar bill, a ten dollar bill, a twenty dollar bill. Add a penny and you're ready for a great demonstration in how easily we can be confused even though we attempt to be diligent.

To begin the routine, you (playing the part of the customer) must have the ten dollar bill and a one dollar bill. It is important at the beginning of the routine that you let the training group understand that you are beginning with eleven dollars.

The rest of the money is given to the volunteer-cashier to make change. Lay that money out on a table in the front of the training room.

You approach the spectator to buy an item that costs 99 cents. Have fun here and pick a funny item to use. Pay for the item with your ten dollar bill. The spectator gives you a penny back and you turn to leave.

She will stop you indicating that you have more change coming. Act surprised but take the

change she now gives you (a $5 bill and four $1 bills).

Suddenly, you realize that you have taken most of the change. Apologize and give her back the $5 bill and four $1 bills suggesting that she give you back the ten dollar bill.

Go ahead and take the $10 bill from the table (cash register) suggesting that she count the money you gave her.

When she tells you that you only gave her nine dollars, apologize and make another suggestion. She's holding nine dollars and you have eleven dollars in your hand. What if you gave her your eleven dollars. Then she would have twenty dollars and could just give you the twenty dollar bill.

Without waiting for her to answer, go ahead and give her the eleven dollars you have and take the twenty dollar bill.

You have just entered the store with eleven dollars, purchased an item and left with twenty dollars! Not bad!

Take time to let the group brainstorm on just when the scam took place. Finally, go through the routine again slowly until the moment of the scam becomes apparent.

This demonstration never fails to astonish a group with how easily our minds can be confused! Good reminder!

COINCIDENTALLY!

This trick uses ten large cards made from pieces of poster board capable of carrying any message desired by the trainer.

A volunteer is brought to the front of the room and given five cards—being told to put the cards behind his back.

The trainer does likewise with his five cards.

Each removes one card from the cards behind his back without looking and hands it to the other person. Each now takes the card he has just been handed and reverses it as he puts it among the cards remaining in his hand.

When the cards are brought out from behind the backs, it is found that both persons chose the exact same card from his five. In fact all of the other cards carry messages exactly the opposite of the two chosen cards.

If the word EXCELLENCE was written on the two cards and MEDIOCRE written all the others, the following segue into the material could easily be used. . .

"Today in this session. . . we will be attempting to locate and identify EXCELLENCE when we see it. We will attempt to lift it above work we would only call MEDIOCRE!"

Prepare ten cards from card stock approximately mately 5"x 7".

On two of those cards print the same positive quality. On the other eight cards print the same negative quality.

In presenting this most puzzling demonstration, invite a volunteer to join you in the front of the room and give her five cards facedown—asking her to put them immediately behind her back without looking at the cards.

You put the other five behind your back.

IMPORTANT: MAKE SURE THAT YOU HAVE BOTH OF THE POSITIVE QUALITY CARDS AMONG YOUR FIVE CARDS AND THAT YOU KNOW WHICH ONES THEY ARE!

Ask your volunteer to hand you any card facedown from her five cards, and you will hand her one of yours too. Hand her one of your positive quality cards.

Now instruct your volunteer to turn over the card you gave her behind her back and place it in the middle of her other facedown cards. You will do the same.

However, you don't exactly do the same. Instead, you will simply place the card she gave you among your cards and will take the other positive quality card—turning it faceup and putting it into the middle of your other cards.

When you both bring out your cards and fan them facedown, you will both have the exact same card turned faceup!

The trainees will immediately be suspicious that all of the cards are the same since you never really showed the other cards!

"I know what you're thinking," you say. "The other cards might be all the same too! You're right! They are!"

At this point, show that all of the cards have a negative quality on them. The two of you have found the only two positive quality cards among the ten!

Congratulate your volunteer and proceed to find and build on their positive qualities too!

TRICKS FOR TRAINERS II

SECTION TWO

Propless Magic For Trainers

These TEN tricks require items that are not prepared
and can quite often be borrowed from members of the
training group.

Section Two

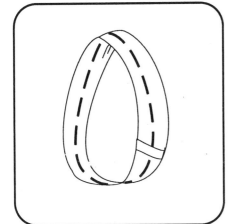

Loop A

Loop B

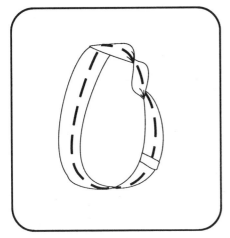

Loop C

SCISSORS RACE

A contest is held between two members of the training class for a truly great prize. The prize could even be a new car! Each is given an adding machine paper strip scotch taped into a long circular ring. The goal is to cut around the ring separating the initial ring into two separate rings. The first one to do just that without tearing their paper wins the car! The trainer first demonstrates and then begins the race. However, at the end of the race one person ends up with two rings linked together and the other finishes with one giant ring! No one wins the prize, but everyone learns a little bit more about examining the situation before jumping in!

The secret to this fun exercise is how you make the paper rings!

Get a roll of adding paper from an adding machine and cut three lengths of paper approximately 10 feet long and 3-4 inches wide.

Make sure you have no twists in the paper when you scotch tape the first one into a circle. This is the paper circle that the trainer will use to demonstrate *(Loop A)*.

When you make the second ring, give the paper a half twist before taping the ends together. This one you will give to one of the contestants *(Loop B)*.

When you make the second ring, give the paper
a full twist before taping the ends together. This
one you will also give to one of the contestants
(Loop C).

In presenting the race, the trainer demonstrates
by cutting around the diameter of the paper circle
neatly cutting the circle into two separate circles.

However, when the contestants attempt to do the
same, they will find that one gets a large single
circle while the other one gets two interlocking
circles!

The rules state that the end result must look like
the trainer's (i.e. two separate paper circles)!

Since no one ever wins the prize, don't be afraid
to make it substantial!

HATS. . . HATS . . .HATS!

Using a single piece of newspaper, the trainer tells a story of a small boy who would play for days with just such a piece of paper. The paper is folded into a series of hats, a ship, and finally a shirt as the story unfolds. It's an inspiring story whose creativity always intrigues a training group!

In learning this creative routine, for ease of handling, it is best to use a smaller tabloid sheet of paper (about 15"x 22").

Before working on the story poem at the end of this routine, learn to make the basic hats. In actual performance you will want to pre-fold the paper so that you can make the folds easily and quickly in front of an audience.

Begin by laying the paper out flat folding it in half each way opening it out flat again as in (figure 1).

Then folding the top half of the paper down so it is even with the bottom half, (figure 2).

Fold the upper left and upper right panels in toward the center, (figure 3). Fold up AB in front, (figure 4). Then fold CD up in back to the position shown in (figure 5). Fold down A and B in front, (figure 6). Then fold down C and D in back, (figure 7).

Bring AC and BD together, (figure 8). The hat will fold flat, (figure 9). Fold B up in the direction of the arrow in (figure 10). Put on the hat.

This is the first hat in the poem THE FIREMAN (*figure 11&12*)!

Take the hat off and fold it flat folding up the backside of the hat in the same manner as the front was folded up for the fireman (*figure 13*). Put the hat on your head sideways and you will look like Napoleon. This is the second hat in the poem THE GENERAL (*figure 14*)!

Turn the hat on your head so that instead of the points being out to the sides they are now in the front and the back. This is the third hat in the poem. You are looking at the hat of a SHIP'S CAPTAIN (*figure 15*).

Take off the hat. Fold in the ends as in (*figure 16*). The hat will then look like (*figure 17*). Grasp A,C, in your left hand and B,D in your right hand. Pull them in opposite directions. The newspaper will open out in the boat pictured in (*figure 18*). This is also spoken of in the poem.

When the storm comes in the poem, you'll demonstrate by tearing off the front as in (*figure 19*), the backside as in (*figure 20*) and the top as in (*figure 21*).

Now when you open out the newspaper you will have a shirt like in (*figure 22*) finishing the poem exactly.

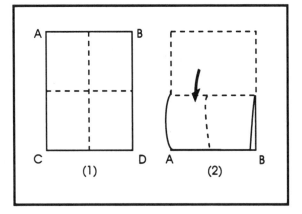

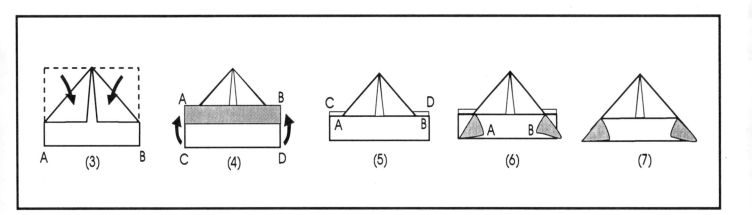

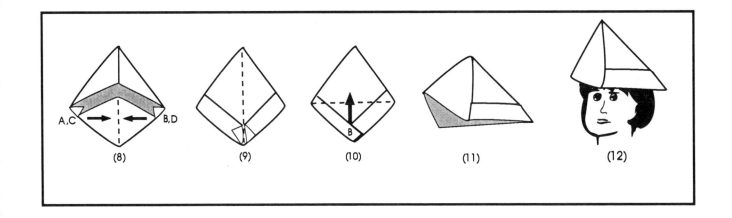

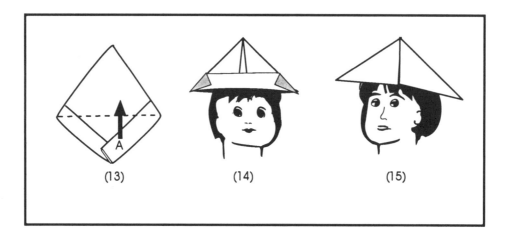

(13)   (14)   (15)

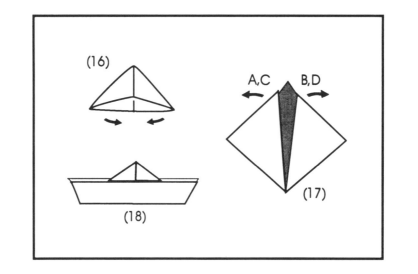

(16)

A,C   B,D

(17)

(18)

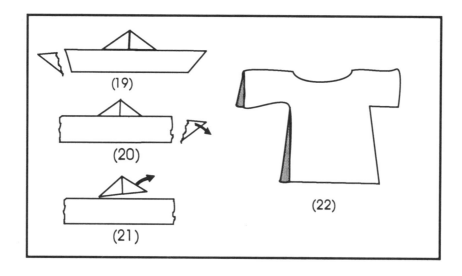

(19)

(20)

(21)

(22)

The Dream Game

The boy was poor
It was plain to see
By the clothes that he wore
By the hole in his knee.

But he'd come to show me a game that he'd play.
The Dream Game he called it. Day after day
A piece of old newspaper he would fold
And with his paper this story he told.

"Don't you see, Mr/s. Trainer," the young man said.
"I could be a fireman with this upon my head.
Or if I turn it this way a General I become
With armies to command and battles to be won.

Or the captain of a giant ship upon a mighty sea
With lots and lots of passengers—one thousand
ninety three.
And if my ship should ever get in trouble with a
storm
I'd try my best to work and keep every single
passenger warm.

In fact you know what I think I could do?
Now, you may not want to bet.
But I believe we'd get to shore
Without my shirt being wet.

"Don't you see, Mr/s. Trainer," the young boy said
to me.
"With this piece of paper and my mind I'll
become what I want to be."

Each time I wad up a piece of paper just to throw
it away
I wonder about that little boy and where he
might be today.
You know . . . I believe that little boy just might
be a King!
For I am very sure he could have become just
about anything!

THE TISSUE TRICK

The trainer claims that she has just learned a new magic trick that uses a tissue. Slowly she tears the tissue and clumsily switches the pieces for another tissue—claiming to have restored the tissue. However during the trick, the group can't help but notice that during the switch the actual pieces have now fallen from her hand to the floor. Not to worry! She picks up the fallen pieces and restores them too!

An added bonus idea is given using a piece of tissue paper with customized content printed on the paper!

To prepare for this trick, roll two pieces of tissue into small balls and place them into your right pants or coat pocket.

Place another piece of tissue (unrolled) into your left pants or coat pocket and you're ready to begin.

Reach into both pockets at the same time and remove the tissue from your left pocket first waving it in the air as you shake it open.

Also, secretly remove the two tissue balls from your right pocket hiding them as best you can in that hand. It's alright if the audience begins to suspect something is in that hand.

Use both hands to tear the piece of open tissue into small pieces rolling them into a ball.

Place the ball into the top of your closed right hand in the opening closest to your thumb. Magically, wave your left hand over the right hand and then using that left hand remove one of the small secret balls from the opening of your right hand closest to your little finger. Act as though these are the pieces restored.

Dramatically open this previously secret ball—indicating by your attitude that you have magically restored the tissue.

While you are opening up this tissue, let the second secret ball fall from your right hand as though it were an accident. Act embarrassed and quickly step on the fallen ball as though to hide it from view. The audience will believe that the tissue now on the floor are the torn pieces you were hiding in your hand.

In your embarrassment, quickly crumple up the open piece of tissue in your hands—roll it up along with the torn pieces still being held in your right hand. Place this packet away in your pocket and turn all your attention to the tissue under your foot.

Reach down and pick up that tissue from the floor. Due to the fact that your foot has smashed it, there is no way for the audience to tell if the packet is the torn pieces or not.

Make a magic gesture over the supposedly torn pieces and open out the tissue to show that they are restored too!

An ADDITIONAL FOR APPLICATION has you introducing your subject by telling your trainees that you want to show them a little magic you've been practicing.

By using pieces of colored tissue paper instead of tissue, you can print words on the paper to help communicate your message. By way of example, you could tear up a piece of paper with the word "MEDIOCRE" on it (indicating your desire to rid the company of all such work). As you restore it, the paper now reads "QUALITY!" The pieces you pick up off the floor have the words "WE CAN DO IT!" boldly printed on it!

You've introduced your subject with an attention grabbing piece of magic!

Tricks for Trainers II   **77**

BUSTED!

Again the trainer claims to have mastered a magic trick using a large empty grocery sack and a balloon that completely fills the inside of the sack. The inflated balloon is placed into the sack. The trainer will now attempt to run a long needle through the outside of the sack through the balloon and out the other side of the sack without hurting the balloon at all!

Slowly the needle is inserted. Suddenly, a loud noise signifies that the balloon has broken! Oh well, the trainer exclaims, "I always carry a spare!" Another completely inflated balloon is now removed from inside the sack!

With a magic marker, words can be printed on the balloons to enhance content delivery!

This most startling demonstration needs to be done with black or dark purple round balloons. They should be as large as possible so that you can just barely get one of them into a large grocery sack. The size of the balloon will depend upon the size of the sack.

Use the eraser end of a pencil to push one of the inflated balloons inside the other. Begin by inflating the inside balloon so that it completely fills the outside balloon. Tie the inside balloon tightly and then inflate the outside balloon so that there is a pocket of air between the inside balloon and outside balloon. Now you can tie off the outside balloon.

This special double balloon is presented to the audience as though it were a single balloon. You begin to brag about a great magic trick you've been practicing. If you brag enough, the audience will begin to want you to fail.

Unfold an empty grocery sack and show it empty. Place the balloon into the bag with the tied end at the top opening of the sack.

Tell the audience that you will now insert the needle (a long thin knitting needle works fine) through the paper sack and through the balloon without breaking the balloon.

Reach into the sack and hold the balloon by the tied end. Insert the needle into the sack while pulling up on the tied end of the outside balloon. Have the needle prick the outside balloon up at the extended neck on which you are pulling and you will hear a loud POP! Remove the pieces of balloon and look discouraged.

Suddenly, get an inspiration. You always carry a spare! Reach into the sack and triumphantly remove the extra balloon!

By writing words on the balloons with either a white grease pencil or mailing label and magic marker, you can emphasize specific content! By popping the balloon marked MEDIOCRE it could be replaced with the balloon labeled QUALITY! Anytime you're desiring to substitute one quality for another, this dramatic demonstration will make it memorable!

figure 1

Fold in half

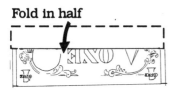

figure 2

Fold in half

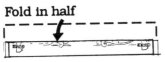

figure 3

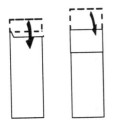

figure 4 & 5

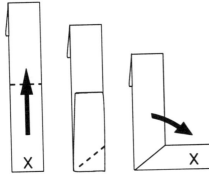

figure 6, 7 & 8

MONEY TO WEAR

Great for use when emphasizing cost control or for building a sense of being #1 in an industry! Each person is given a one dollar bill to wear on their finger! That's right! The bill is folded into a perfectly shaped ring with the number ONE right on top in the signet position! They look great and helps to bring a group together. The dollar bill is only folded. It is not torn or mutilated in any way!

Here's how to make this unique ring!

Use as crisp a dollar bill as possible. Make sure the creases are sharp. Begin by holding the bill with Washington's picture uppermost. Fold in the upper and lower white borders, (figure 1).

Fold the top half down, (figure 2). Then fold the bill in half again, (figure 3). Turn the bill lengthwise and fold down the white border of the bill as in (figure 4). then fold down the top ¾", (figure 5).This is the portion with the word "one." The "ONE" will later be the setting in the ring.

Turn the bill over, (figure 6) and fold the bottom 2" up in the direction of the arrow. The result is shown in (figure 7). We will refer to this 2" section as flap X. If this section is folded longer than 2" the ring will fit a smaller finger. A few tries will show you how to size the ring by the length of this flap X.

Fold flap X along the dotted diagonal line in (figure 7) to the position shown in (figure 8).

Turn the bill around and place it against your left forefinger, *(figure 9)*. The top section of the bill is brought around behind your forefinger and up in front, in the direction of the arrows. The result to this point is shown in *(figure 10)*.

With the bill in the position of *(figure 10)*, release the portion with the "ONE" so that it flips up, *(figure 11)*. Now bring flap X over to the right in the direction of the arrow in *(figure 11)*. The result is shown in *(figure 12)*.

Bring the portion with the setting down in the direction of the arrow in *(figure 12)*. The white margin is then tucked in as shown in *(figure 13)*. Flap X is then brought inside the ring and tucked into the diagonal pocket shown in *(figure 14)*. The result is the ring shown in *(figure 15)*.

figure 9

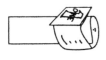
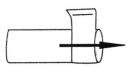

figure 10 & 11

figure 12 & 13

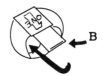

figure 14 & 15

DOUBLE EXPOSURE

Imagine taking a Polaroid picture of your training group only to have a summary word or statement mysteriously appear in the picture—floating above their heads! They'll talk about this one for a long time!

There's a little known fact about the older Polaroid cameras that you can exploit in this unbelievable demonstration!

First, you'll need to find one of the older cameras in which you would manually pull out the picture and develop it OUTSIDE of the camera. The Colorpak II was one of the more popular versions of this brand and can still be found in second hand stores and garage sales.

If you take a picture with this type of camera and leave the picture in the camera (not pulling it out to develop it), the next picture you take with the camera will double expose itself over the first one still in the camera!

So. . . before you take the picture of your training group, lay a black piece of material on the ground and put a message sign at the top edge of that material. The sign should be white with black letters describing a final summary statement you can use to conclude your training.

Load your camera with a black and white film
pack and take a flash picture of the dark material and sign. The dark material and the sign
should fill your viewfinder. Be sure and position
the sign in the picture so that it is at the very top
of the picture.

Now don't pull the picture out of the camera.

When you use this camera to take a picture of
your training group, you will find a neat little
sign with your summary message right in the
picture—across the top of your group picture!
It's spooky! It's unreal! It's definitely memorable!

84   Tricks for Trainers II

FLASH!

Holding a flashcube in her otherwise empty hand, the trainer moves around the room with this "portable volunteer finder." Suddenly, as she approaches one of the trainees, there is a bright flash as one of the bulbs ignite. This process can be repeated with all four of the bulbs in the flashcube if desired. Or use it as an energizer with the group holding hands and rubbing their feet on the floor until the static electricity causes the bulb to ignite! Great fun!

Purchase a box of disposable FLASHCUBES. They must be the flashcubes that flash four times. Don't buy a flash bar, since it won't work!

As you look at the bottom of the flashcube, you will see four curved slots. Across the middle of each slot inside the flashcube is a very very thin piece of wire.

That wire is the trigger for the flashcube! Anything you press against the wire will cause that particular flashbulb to ignite!

Take a pair of scissors and cut a wedge of eraser off the end of a pencil. If you insert that wedge of eraser into one of the slots and press it against the wire, the flash will ignite. However, you don't want to do that just yet!

Instead, just gently insert the eraser until it just
touches the wire and you're ready to amaze your
trainees!

When the time is right, pick up the flashcube and
hold it between your index finger and thumb
with your thumb resting on the piece of eraser.

If you decide to use it as a group energizer, wait
until the group is rubbing its feet at a feverish
pitch and then use your thumb to push against
the eraser!

FLASH! Your group will stumble back to their
seats in amazement as little lights dance in front
of their eyes!

86   Tricks for Trainers II

STEP RIGHT UP ! !

Don't just point to someone when you need a volunteer. Select them by magic! Four large cards (patterns supplied in the book) are used with words printed on each card. When the cards are selected and then read in order, they say "LET'S HAVE SOMEONE VOLUNTEER. . . THAT'S A GOOD IDEA! . . . WHO WILL DO IT? . . . I WILL!" Even though the selection looks random, the trainer actually has complete control over who gets the final "I WILL" card. A great joke to pull on that fun-loving person in the training group.

Make copies of cards #1, #2, #3, & #6 from this book.

Have them printed onto card stock and laminated if you plan to use this a lot!

When you need a volunteer, decide who'll be fun for what you have in mind and introduce the four cards with their backs to the audience.

Card #6 is the force card and should be one of the middle two cards when the four cards are fanned for a selection.

Go first to the person you want to volunteer and ask him for a number between one and four. Say it boldly and it won't be analyzed.

Needless to say the only two numbers possible
are 2 or 3. Count from either the right end or the
left end of the fan so that the first person gets the
force card #6.

Now, have any other person state which card she
wants by saying either 1, 2, or 3. Count to their
selected card and give it to them.

Then have someone else give you either number
1 or 2 and give them their selected card.

Finally, give away the remaining card to the final
volunteer.

Each person will read the message on their card
beginning with #1 . . . then #2 . . . then #3 . . .
and finally #6.

The person reading card #6 has indeed volunteered.

This will not seem like a magic trick to the
trainees until you use **Step Right Up II** later in
the session. Then they will see that all isn't what
it appears.

#2

THAT'S
A GOOD
IDEA!

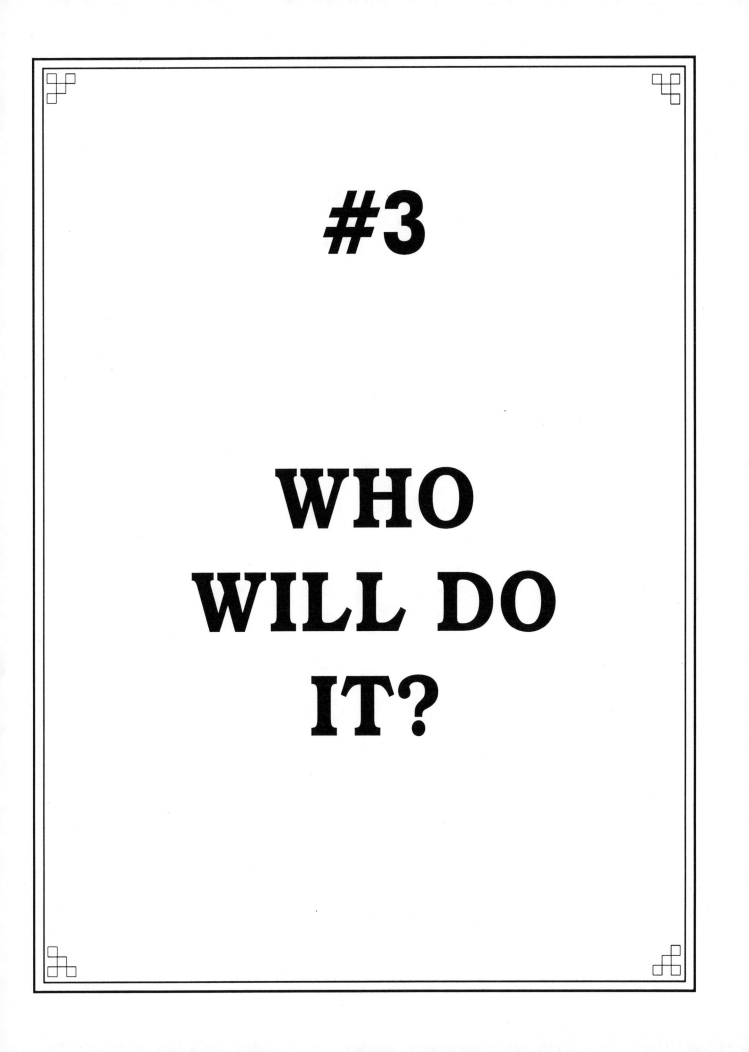

#3

WHO WILL DO IT?

#4

NOT
ME!

STEP RIGHT UP II!

After you've used "Step Right Up I," use this one by adding two more cards to the four used before! The same person still gets the volunteer card! He'll know he's being picked on now!

Similar to STEP RIGHT UP I except that this version uses SIX cards.

Make a copy of all six cards found in this book— printing them onto card stock and laminating them if you plan to use this game frequently in your training.

As in Step Right Up I, the sixth card is the force card and should be forced again on the volunteer you used in Step Right Up I.

In order to get him to take the force card, place card #6 third card in from the end of the fan as you fan the cards with their backs towards the audience.

Ask the person you want to get card #6 to pick any number from 1-6. Depending upon what number he states, you do the following to make sure he gets the card #6 (the third card in from the end).

Start from the end of the fan counting towards
card #6—tapping one card at a time.

1.....................Spell O-N-E giving
        him card #6

2.....................Spell T-W-O giving him card #6

3.....................Count 1-2-3 giving him card #6

4.....................Count from the other end of the fan
        1-2-3-4, he gets #6

5.....................Spell from this same end of the fan
        F-I-V-E, he gets #6

6.....................Spell from the original end of the fan
        S-I-X, he gets #6

Each of these processes will have the first
spectator landing on card #6.

Now have the others give you numbers and count
to their selection until all of the cards have been
distributed.

Finally, have the volunteers read their cards in
order from 1-6. The group will laugh as they
realize you've selected the same trainee again!

DIVIDE AND DECIDE!

This is an apparently random way of giving away a prize to one of the trainees. Even though there are six very expensive prizes and one inexpensive prize, the trainee always get the inexpensive prize!

The supposed fairness of this game is found in the title of "Divide and Decide." If a pie was being cut and shared between two parties, the fairest possible way to divide the pie and distribute the pieces would be for one person to cut it into the two pieces and then the other person decide which piece each party received.

Although this game appears to adhere to that most fair system, you will soon see that the game is always under the control of the trainer. She decides which prize is finally won by the trainee!

Take seven index cards and print a different prize on each index card. Make the prizes fabulous on six of the cards, since you'll never ever give them away. You might offer a new car, stereo, entertainment center, boat, cruise, cash, etc.

On the seventh card, make sure you list a prize that you are prepared to award.

Even though the cards will be shuffled and placed face down on a table in the front of the room, you as the trainer must always know which card has the inexpensive prize. Make a small mark on the back of this card so that you can identify it at all times.

THE TRAINER MUST ALWAYS BEGIN with the excuse of showing the trainee how the game is played. The trainer places her hands on top of two prize cards. The trainee decides which of the two cards (being touched by the trainer) will be eliminated. The eliminated card is then read so that everyone knows which prize the trainee has failed to win.

RULE #1: The trainer NEVER places his hand on the inexpensive prize card when it is her turn to touch two of the prizes!

Then the trainee touches two prizes and the trainer decides which one is to be eliminated. This card is read to see which prize the trainee has failed to win now!

RULE #2: The trainer NEVER has the trainee remove the inexpensive prize card when she selects the prize to be eliminated.

As long as the trainer adheres to the two rules stated above, the inexpensive prize card will be the one remaining after the others have been eliminated.

TRICKS FOR TRAINERS II

SECTION THREE

Teach Them A Trick

The following TWELVE magic tricks are designed to be performed and then taught to the members of the training class to help emphasize a point with hands-on involvement.

INVISIBLE BALL TRICK

With a paper lunch sack and their imaginations, the trainees will be doing "invisible ball juggling" in no time! With a little musical background, it's great fun as they actually hear the balls land in their sacks!

What a fun imagination energizer this becomes!

Pass out lunch sacks to everyone in the group and ask them to open them up and fold down the top as though there really was something inside the sack. Have them open the top of their sack, reach in and pretend to take out a ball about the size of a ping pong ball. Have them hold it up so that others can see. While they continue to hold theirs, throw your ball in the air, watch it with your eyes and then have it land in your sack with a loud THUD!

The secret to making the sound is to hold your sack between your two "snapping fingers." Usually these fingers would be the tip of your thumb and your middle finger. Hold the paper of the sack deep in the crotch of your thumb and snap your fingers. If you slightly drop your arm at the same time this snap is made, the illusion is perfect that something has landed in your sack!

You can bounce it off the ceiling and catch it in your sack! You can bounce it off the wall and catch it in your sack!

You can even bring two people to the front of the room, add a little music and watch your "invisible ball juggling" routine with one tossing it to the other and then back and forth again! Your group will have much fun experimenting with the possibilities!

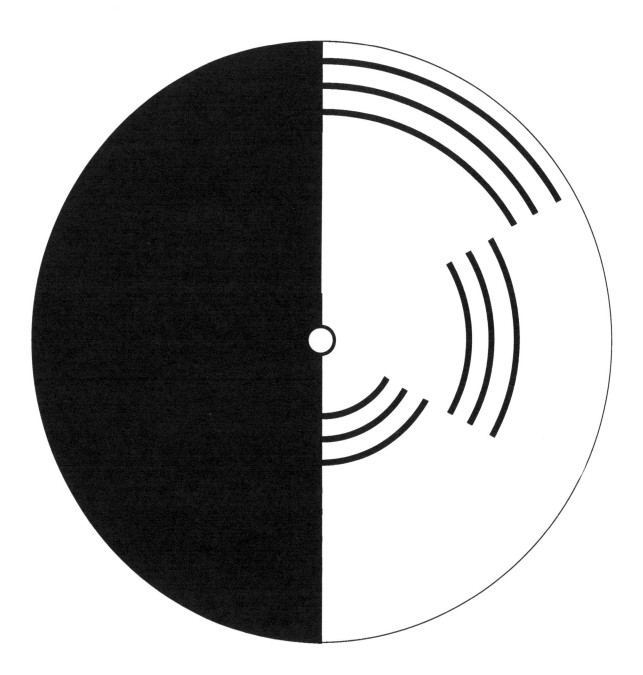

RAINBOW WHEEL

This black and white wheel can be made into a top by inserting a short pencil through the center hole. Then when it's spun on the tabletop, colors appear in the wheel. It's great for illustrating how we can often see the positive in situations if we just look closely enough!

Reduce the pattern supplied to make a wheel for each person in your training class. A wheel with about a 3 ½" diameter works well. Use heavy white posterboard stock for best results.

When a sharpened golf pencil is pushed through the center hole, the circle can be spun on a table just like a top. However, the most interesting phenomena occurs. Even though the wheel is clearly only black and white, colors appear in the wheel!

You might also want to consider using the graphic in its present size. Make a copy on white paper and then glue the paper to a piece of cardboard backing. Insert and attach this wheel to the end of a drill bit inserted into an electric drill (with variable speed).

Now you can rotate the wheel so that several people at once will be able to see the colors!

The application is graphic! When we look closely with a positive outlook, we can usually see some color in even the most drab situation!

CHALLENGE VANISH

The trainer places any content oriented item under a handkerchief. Group members feel the item under the handkerchief. Suddenly, the trainer whips the handkerchief away and the item is gone! The handkerchief may be examined! When this one is explained to the group, many applications present themselves.

Any small item (possibly even representational of content under discussion) is placed under an opaque handkerchief.

The trainer holds it through the handkerchief and allows members of the training class to reach under the handkerchief and actually feel the object to prove that it's still there.

The trainer returns to the front of the room and suddenly whisks the handkerchief away! The item is GONE!

How did it happen?

The class brainstorms on the possibilities before the trainer explains. The last student to feel under the handkerchief is a secret accomplice arranged beforehand! This student actually removes the item from under the handkerchief. However, the trainer continues to hold the handkerchief as though it is still there.

Upon returning to the front of the room, the vanish comes as a complete surprise to everyone in the class (well. . .ok . . . almost everyone in the class)!

OVERHEAD!

One of the trainees leaves the room so he cannot see what's happening in the room but remains within listening distance. The trainer moves around the room holding her hand above different members' heads and saying simply the word "overhead." Then she stops and says "Over whose head?" and the out-of-the-room trainee correctly names the person where the trainer has stopped. This is repeated until someone in the group begins to figure out how it's done! This one really requires great observational skills!

The description pretty well tells the effect of this most puzzling demonstration.

Prior to the performance, the trainer and his assistant have arranged that the trainer will say the words "Over whose head" only when he is standing with his hand over the head OF THE LAST PERSON TO SPEAK JUST BEFORE THE ASSISTANT LEAVES THE ROOM!

This system works great particularly when the assistant stands by the door and leaves immediately after someone makes a comment!

The group will go crazy trying to figure out the system. It takes great observational attention to detail.

This demonstration could actually be done several times throughout the course of a day until someone begins to discover the pattern.

A LITTLE HELP FROM MY FRIENDS

This time several trainees are led from the room and brought back in one by one as the trainer presents a magic trick with the help of others in the group. Eventually, the trainees begin to catch on to how the magic is done and the importance of observation is underscored again!

This demonstration differs from the previously described presentation entitled OVERHEAD! since in this version the entire group knows how the magic is done with the exception of the two or three volunteers who are brought into the room to participate in the demonstration.

On a small table in the front of the training room is a table, three coffee cups, and any item small enough to fit completely under one of the coffee cups.

As one volunteer at a time is brought into the room, the trainer turns her back and asks that volunteer to place the small item under any of the cups on the table.

She turns around and time and time again correctly identifies which cup the item has been placed under!!!

The secret is simple and bold. When the volunteers are still out of the room, the trainer explains that each person in the training group is to sit with the left eye closed if the item is placed under the left cup, the right eye closed if the item is placed under the right cup, and both eyes

open if the item is placed under the middle cup.

With only a quick glance at the group, the trainer will know under which cup the volunteer has placed the item. The trainer should immediately draw all attention to the cups and away from the audience as she passes her hand over the cups, etc. to discern the correct cup.

Do this several times before telling the volunteer how it's done. Then the volunteer can sit and watch the next one come in and repeat the process.

Take time at the end to analyze why it was difficult for the volunteer to spot the rather obvious method to the trick.

Observation of details and the focus of the attention would certainly be two essential ingredients that make this trick possible. Can you find others?

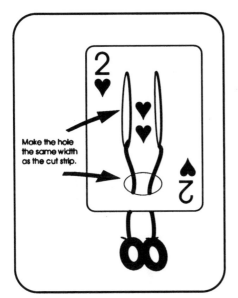

Make the hole the same width as the cut strip.

GENIUS TEST

Made from a playing card, a string and two washers, this puzzle challenges the most creative as they seek to remove the washers without damaging the card! Great for encouraging creative problem solving!

The secret is shown at a glance in the drawing.

To set up the apparatus, bend the top of the card down, then pull the paper strip through the hole as shown. Thread the washers through the strip, then straighten the apparatus. The result is shown.

When a volunteer gives up trying to free the rings, put the puzzle out of sight turning your back. Then show him that the rings are removed!

Finally demonstrate how the puzzle is solved—taking time to analyze what makes it difficult to figure out.

The trainees will find that they have limited themselves with rules of their own making in seeking to solve this puzzle! We do it all the time in many different situations!

COUNTING SHEEP

No matter how slowly the trainer states the question, the group has trouble understanding what he's trying to say. Great for working on communication and listening skills!

Say the following sentence to your group and ask them for the correct answer:

"A man had twenty sick (26) sheep. One sheep died. How many sheep did he have left?"

When presenting the problem to the class, verbally tie together the words "twenty sick sheep" without breaking between the words "sick" and "sheep." Even without hurrying those words, it will sound to your audience like you said "twenty-six sheep."

When the class responds to your question with the answer of "25," tell them that the answer is wrong and offer to repeat the problem again.

When you're ready for them to guess what's happening, tell them that the correct answer is really "19" and repeat the problem again.

Finally, someone will figure it out! The explanation emphasizes the importance of good communication skills in creating a successful problem solving environment.

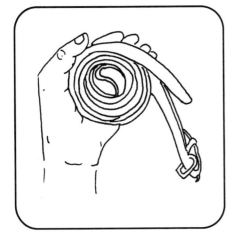

WIN! WIN!

Using an old carnival game, the trainer illustrates the nature of a win-win negotiation!

This is a great demonstration of an old carnival game. Many unknowing people had their money taken by this swindle.

Double a belt in half and then roll it. Have a spectator attempt to find the true center loop by inserting a pencil into the loop—holding both ends of the pencil securely in his hands. Now if you pull on the two ends of the belt, the belt will catch on the pencil if he chose the true center loop. The belt will fall away from the pencil if he didn't catch the right loop.

Here is how to always be in a position where you control the outcome of this innocent-appearing game. When you double the belt make sure that the buckle side is a little longer than the other end of the belt.

Then roll the belt so that the buckle end is on the inside of the other end when the rolling is completed. Now have the spectator insert the pencil. If he guesses wrongly (you'll know by simply paying attention as you roll the belt), simply pull on the two ends of the belt, and the belt will fall free from the pencil.

If he should happen to guess correctly, release the tip of the belt (without the buckle), and it will swing around to the buckled end.

Then pull both ends of the belt, and the belt will fall away from the pencil.

You can make it so that the person will either win or lose as you desire.

At first, when no money was involved, the carnival operator would make it so that the spectator would always win. This would build the spectator's confidence in his abilities to make money with the game.

You can teach this to your trainees as a perfect example of creating a win-win situation. Teach them how to make the spectator a winner no matter what choice he makes.

They'll have fun with this one!

PSYCHIC CONTENT REVIEW

This mindreading trick can be customized to any content review (thirty questions). As the trainees work the trick on each other, they are actually reviewing the material!

This fun method for review actually teaches your trainees a magic trick while they review up to thirty questions of content!

Make a list of thirty questions that will summarize the content you'll be teaching.

Use six 4" x 6" index cards and head one of the cards with the word 'QUESTIONS.' Type the thirty questions on the front and back of this card numbering the questions 1-30. It will look something like below:

QUESTIONS

1. Define the term "role play."
2. Describe a simulation game.
3. Explain an Early Bird Exercise.
4. Etc.
5. Etc.
6. Etc.

Number each of the other five cards at the top of the card #1, #2, #3, #4, #5. On these five index cards, type only some of the (30) questions on each card. The pattern below tells you which numbered questions you will type on each card.

HOWEVER, DO NOT NUMBER THE QUESTIONS ON THESE
INDEX CARDS. SIMPLY TYPE OUT THE QUESTION ITSELF.
Now make as many copies of your cards as you have students
in your training class.

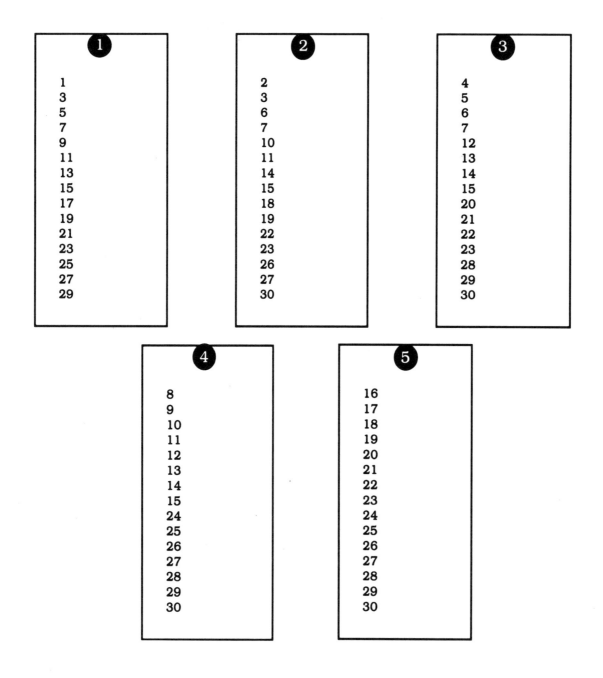

①
1
3
5
7
9
11
13
15
17
19
21
23
25
27
29

②
2
3
6
7
10
11
14
15
18
19
22
23
26
27
30

③
4
5
6
7
12
13
14
15
20
21
22
23
28
29
30

④
8
9
10
11
12
13
14
15
24
25
26
27
28
29
30

⑤
16
17
18
19
20
21
22
23
24
25
26
27
28
29
30

Reproduce it on card stock if at all possible. Cut the individual cards apart so that each person will receive six cards—one master question card and five different numbered cards.

In performing the magic trick, explain that you will be doing a little mindreading trick. Hand the master question card to a volunteer and have her mentally select one question on the card. She is to say nothing. She is only to remember the question she mentally selects.

Now take back the master question card and hand her the other numbered cards one at a time. Have her keep the ones that contain her question. She should give you back any card that does NOT contain her question.

Use the ones she gives you back to figure out which numbered cards she STILL HAS IN HER HANDS. These are the cards that hold the key to figuring out which question she has selected. Have her concentrate hard on her question.

Use the following process to determine her selected question. Here is where the numbers at the top of the cards become important. Each numbered card has an easy to remember value:

Card 1 has a value of 1
Card 2 has a value of 2
Card 3 has a value of 4
Card 4 has a value of 8
Card 5 has a value of 16

Each card is worth twice as much as the one before it. It's easy to remember the values that way!

If your volunteer KEEPS cards numbered 1 & 2, you add the values of those cards as given above (1 + 2), and you will know that she is thinking of question #3 on your master question card.

If your volunteer KEEPS cards numbered 4 & 5, you add the values above (8 + 16), and you will know that she is thinking of question #24 on your master question card.

If your volunteer KEEPS cards numbered 1, 2, & 3, you know that she is thinking of question #7 on your master question card (1 + 2 + 4).

Even though you know the answer, don't answer the question immediately. . . make it dramatic! Get the question letter by letter. . . or a picture in your mind. Only tell her the answer to her question AFTER you've put the master question card and her discarded cards away. Make it seem as though those cards had nothing to do with how the trick works.

Afterwards, pass out the cards so each trainee gets a set and teach them how to do the trick.

For review, have the trainees work with a practice partner and have them think about the ANSWER to the question rather than the question itself. Have each practice partner try it with their partner and then reverse and have the trick done on them. Have them practice in this rotation for a set amount of time.

With technical information, the cards can be designed with actions (i.e. computer training) which the person must successfully complete!

figure 2

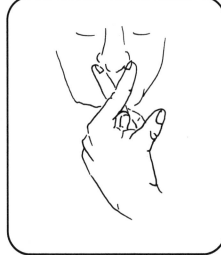

figure 2

FOLLOW THE LEADER

The directions are given slowly by the trainer and even demonstrated. Nevertheless, the group finds it very difficult to successfully complete the action. This works excellently for demonstrating the importance of detailing our communications.

This fun demonstration can be done very slowly and deliberately. Your trainees will still have trouble following your actions! The resulting explanation really helps each person understand the role of assumptions in misunderstandings.

As you show the group what you want them to do, extend both arms directly in front of you—crossing them over one another with the right arm going on top of the left one. Press your hands together open palm against open palm and interlace your fingers SO THAT THE LITTLE FINGER OF YOUR RIGHT HAND IS ON TOP OF THE LITTLE FINGER OF YOUR LEFT HAND (*figure 1*).

This last piece of instruction is very important! Although you never verbally tell your trainees what you are doing, you must always interlace your fingers in this manner. You will find that your trainees will not interlace their fingers in the same way.

Bend your elbows and bring your interlaced fingers through your arms and up to your nose. Without undoing your fingers, simply extend your two index fingers. Leaving them crossed, place one finger alongside each nostril touching

it with the fingernail of that finger *(figure 2)*.

Pressing your index fingers alongside your nose, unlace your other fingers and rotate your hands outward so that everything uncrosses and your right hand is on the right side of your nose and your left hand is on the left side of your nose.

Ask your group to follow you carefully. However due to the fact that in the beginning the interlacing of their fingers will be done incorrectly, they will be unable to untwine their hands at the end of the demonstration! Show them how to do it correctly, and they will realize how important little details can be in our communications!

LIAR! LIAR!

With a television gameshow format, the trainer successfully tells time and time again which of two people is lying in response to his question. The group really interacts as they seek to find the solution to this fun exercise!

The rules are quite simple. . .two volunteers try to stump the trainer!

The two volunteers are given a finger ring and leave the room to discuss and decide two questions:

1) Which one will hide the ring on his person?

2) Which one will be "THE LIAR" and which one will be "THE TRUTHTELLER?"

IMPORTANT: WHEN THEY COME BACK INTO THE ROOM, THE LIAR MUST LIE, AND THE TRUTHTELLER MUST TELL THE TRUTH!

When they re-enter the room, the trainer is allowed to ask only one person one question. Nevertheless he is always able to determine who holds the ring!

This book won't attempt to explain why this trick works, but when the two people come back into the room, the trainer asks:

DOES THE LIAR HAVE THE RING?

The trainer looks for the negative answer about the ring. If, when you ask this question, the person answers "no" then he DOES have the ring. If he answers "yes," then the other person has the ring.

For a variation, you can ask the question:

DOES THE TRUTHTELLER HAVE THE RING?

Now you look for the "yes" answer. If the person you ask answers "yes," then you know he has the ring. If he answers "no," then you know that the other person has the ring.

For yet another variation. . . have both a coin and a ring with one holding one and one holding the other. Determining which has which is still no more difficult. However, you now have four possible questions you can use:

DOES THE LIAR HAVE THE RING?
DOES THE LIAR HAVE THE COIN?
DOES THE TRUTHTELLER HAVE THE RING?
DOES THE TRUTHTELLER HAVE THE COIN?

126   Tricks for Trainers II

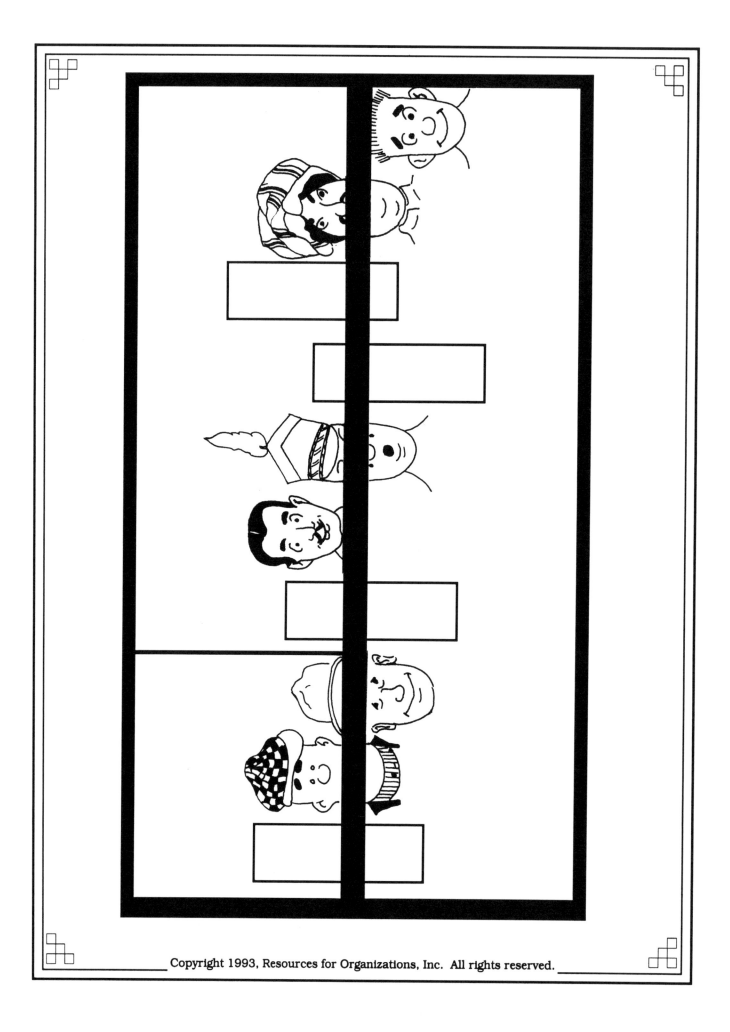

IT'S GONE!

Working with a small puzzle of three pieces, the trainees receive a graphic illustration of the vanishing (or appearing) of a key piece of content. Even though they hold the pieces in their hands and do the magic themselves, this one is not easily explained!

Duplicate the drawing on the opposite page so that each of your trainees has one. Have them notice that there are SIX people and several doors in the picture. Carefully have them cut away all the solid black. They will now have three separate pieces.

After counting the people in the puzzle, have them switch positions of the two shorter pieces on the top half of the puzzle. They will suddenly find that now there are only FIVE people! One of the persons must have left through one of the doors!

This can also be done in reverse by starting with only FIVE people and then having another person appear through one of the doors!

APPLICATION IDEAS include using this to illustrate the type of employee that works best with your company. The doors could be doors into the company itself. They could also be office doors to executive offices (indicating promotion).

The ones consistently promoted are those who _____. You now have a visual demonstration of your main message. Your trainees will take the puzzle, keep it, and show it! Each time your message will be reinforced!

TRICKS FOR TRAINERS II

SECTION FOUR

Early Bird Fun

This section contains SIX audience tested early bird exercises that involve the audience in the material before the seminar even begins.

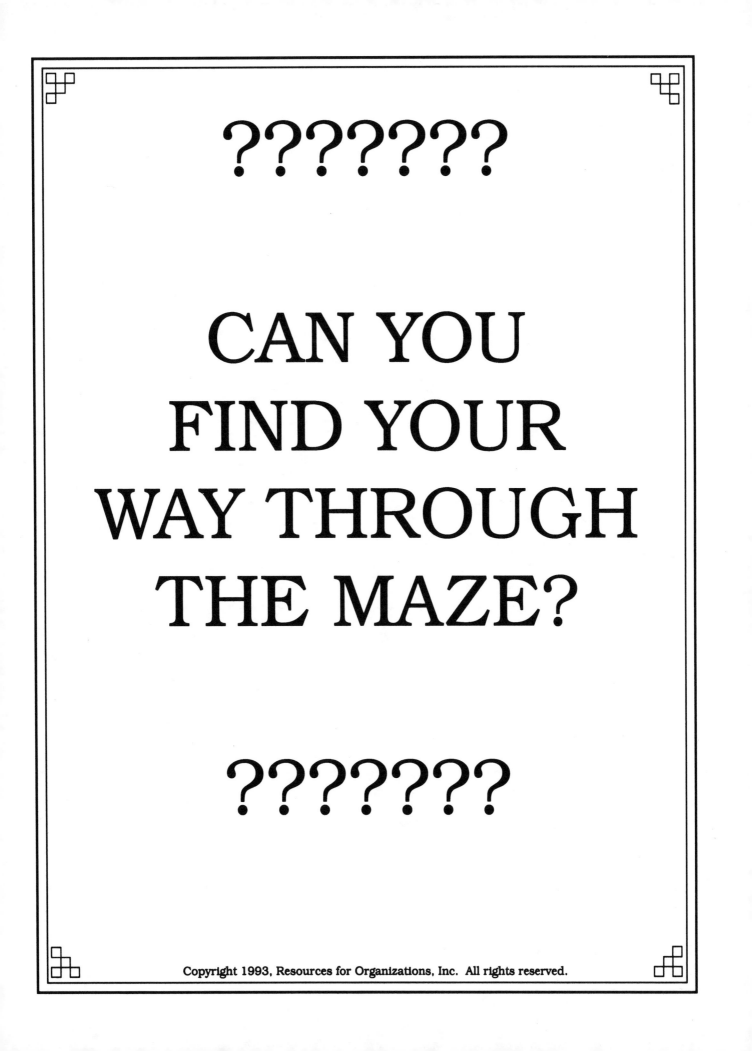

??????

CAN YOU FIND YOUR WAY THROUGH THE MAZE?

??????

START

END

EXERCISE #1

This maze can be customized to content. Comes complete with handout and transparency masters. Can your trainees find their way from the beginning to the end of this challenging maze?

Take the maze on the opposite page and make a copy of it as you prepare to customize it to your content.

You can add words or pictures to the START position (upper left-hand corner), the END position (lower right-hand corner), and the MIDDLE position.

By way of example, if you're training your group in time management, you might have a clock in the middle position with the words "TIME WASTE" at the start position, and the words "EFFECTIVE TIME USE" at the end position.

Make enough copies for each of your trainees and use it as an early bird exercise. It will generate group energy even before the training is ready to begin!

If you also make it up as a transparency, you can demonstrate the route for the group at the conclusion of the exercise!

??????

HOW WOULD YOU ARRANGE THE THREE PIECES SO THAT EACH RIDER SITS ON THE BACK OF A HORSE

??????

EXERCISE #2

This classic puzzle comes with three pieces. Can your trainees arrange the three pieces so that the two jockeys are riding on top of the two horses? Complete with handout and transparency masters.

Duplicate and cut out the following pieces so that each person in your training group has all three.

Then make a transparency from the master on the opposite page.

Your group will generate great energy by working together to solve this classic puzzle. The solution below will help you if you get stuck too!

You might consider making a transparency of the solution too so that you can share it with the group.

THE SOLUTION
Step One

Step Two

EXERCISE #3

Arranging these pieces into a cross isn't as easy as it first seems! Complete with handout and transparency masters.

Duplicate the pieces on the opposite page— cutting them apart so that each person in your group receives all of the pieces. Then make a transparency using the master on the following page.

By also making a transparency of the pieces on the opposite page, you'll be able to share the solution with your training group after they've all given it their best try.

AN ADDITIONAL IDEA might include dividing the group into teams and giving each team only one set of pieces to encourage teamwork and greater interaction.

???????

HOW WOULD
YOU ARRANGE
THE FIVE
PUZZLE
PIECES SO
THAT THEY
FORM A CROSS

???????

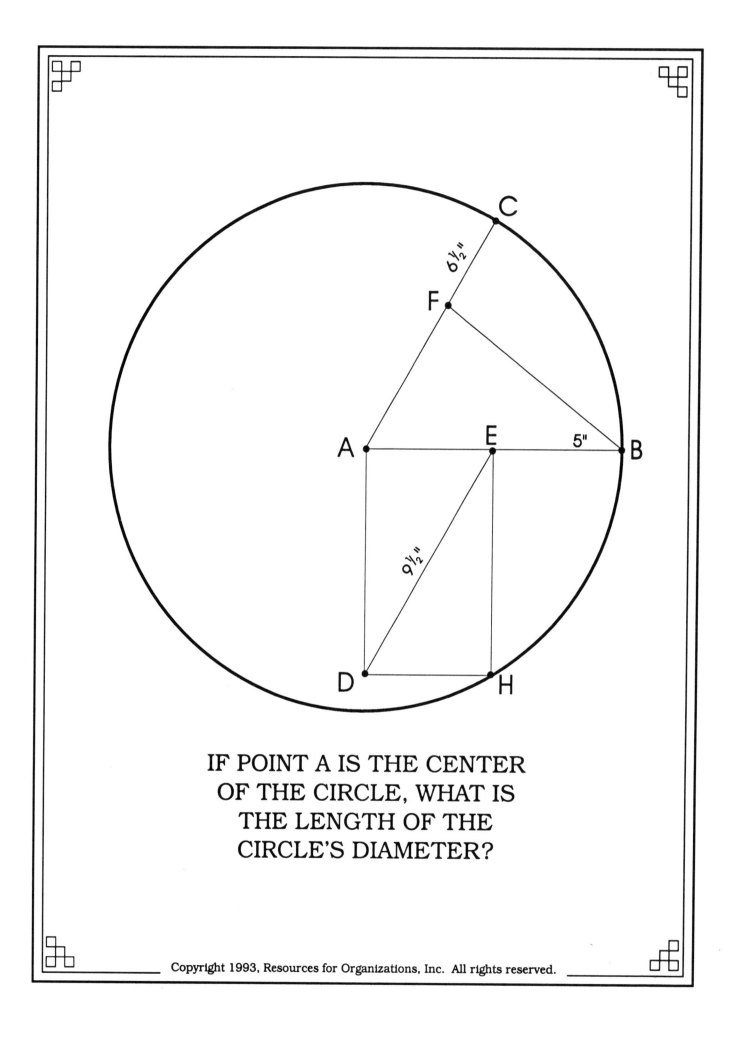

IF POINT A IS THE CENTER
OF THE CIRCLE, WHAT IS
THE LENGTH OF THE
CIRCLE'S DIAMETER?

EXERCISE #4

This puzzle looks like it would take geometry, calculus, or trigonometry to solve! Yet, it's more simple than that as soon as your trainees sift through the unnecessary details. Transparency master included.

Make a transparency from the master on the opposite page and place it on the overhead.

The answer is simple when you focus on the diagonal line in the rectangle at the bottom of the circle. If you draw another diagonal in that rectangle connecting the other corners, you will actually know that the length of the circle's radius is 9 ½" (since the two diagonals in the rectangle will be the same length). Multiply that radius length by two and you'll have the diameter of the circle.

The correct answer is 19".

This puzzle requires a viewer to sift through much information that is superfluous to the actual solving of the question at hand.

Many of the problems we face in life and business require exactly the same process!

???????

HOW COULD YOU CUT A HOLE IN AN INDEX CARD LARGE ENOUGH TO WALK THROUGH IT?

???????

EXERCISE #5

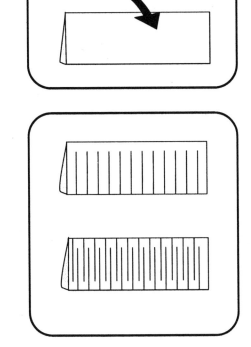

Can your class figure out how to cut a hole in an index card big enough for a full-size person to walk through it? They will be able to once you show them how! Most amazing!

Giving each training team an index card (4" x 6"), encourage them to experiment in using a pair of scissors to cut a hole in the card large enough for a person to walk through it!

The diagram gives you a possible solution.

Fold the card in half. Then open it out and cut a slit along the fold ALMOST from end to end.

Fold the slit card in half again with the slit at the top of the folded card. Then make a number of cuts in the card from the slit down ALMOST to the bottom edge of the card. Don't cut clear through.

Finally make a number of cuts from the bottom edge of the folded card ALMOST to the slit. Don't cut clear through to the slit. Notice how these cuts alternate with the cuts already made. Make the cuts as close together as possible in order to make the biggest possible hole at the end!

Now unfold the card and carefully open it out. Be careful not to tear it. You will find a circle big enough to step through!

Many proposals look impossible when first projected! First impressions can be misleading!

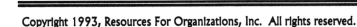

LETTERS OF MYSTERY

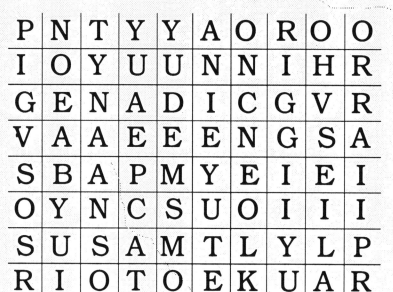

P	N	T	Y	Y	A	O	R	O	O
I	O	Y	U	U	N	N	I	H	R
G	E	N	A	D	I	C	G	V	R
V	A	A	E	E	E	N	G	S	A
S	B	A	P	M	Y	E	I	E	I
O	Y	N	C	S	U	O	I	I	I
S	U	S	A	M	T	L	Y	L	P
R	I	O	T	O	E	K	U	A	R
N	E	R	L	T	G	Y	W	E	A
T	O	A	N	N	H	U	Y	T	T

THESE LETTERS HAVE A SPECIAL MESSAGE JUST FOR YOU!

• Close your eyes and place your fingertip on any letter.

• Open your eyes and write down that letter. Then count five letters to the right writing down that letter. Continue writing down every fifth letter until you get back to the first letter you touched. When you come to the end of a line, continue counting at the left end of the next line. When you reach the bottom of the board, continue counting at the top.

YOUR MESSAGE IS FOUND IN THE LETTERS YOU GET!

EXERCISE #6

Using this ancient-appearing board containing jumbles of letters, group members can follow the instructions and find up to five different messages hidden in the board. These messages may be content oriented. It seems so mysterious when the messages begin to appear!

Before stopping to figure out how to customize one of these Magic Boards for your content, take a moment to follow the directions with the board in this book. This mysterious board will tell you something true about you!

HOW TO CUSTOMIZE THE BOARD

1) Make a copy of the blank grid supplied with this book.

2) Write FIVE sentence messages you want emphasized to your trainees. Each sentence must be composed of exactly TWENTY letters. These sentences can be sentences of truth pertaining to quality, cost control, management principles, attitudes, etc.

3) Starting with the square in the upper left-hand corner of your board, type letters into the boxes placing one letter in every fifth box until you have entered your first sentence into the grid.

4) Then start with the second box from the left in the top row and put in your second sentence using every fifth box.

5) Continue until the grid is full of letters comprising your five key statements.

PURPOSEFULLY we did not title the blank grid so that you could entitle it something pertaining to your content topic.

Some suggestions might include:

The Ancient Management Board Of Counsel

The Mysterious Financial Oracle

Your Positive Strength Magic Chart

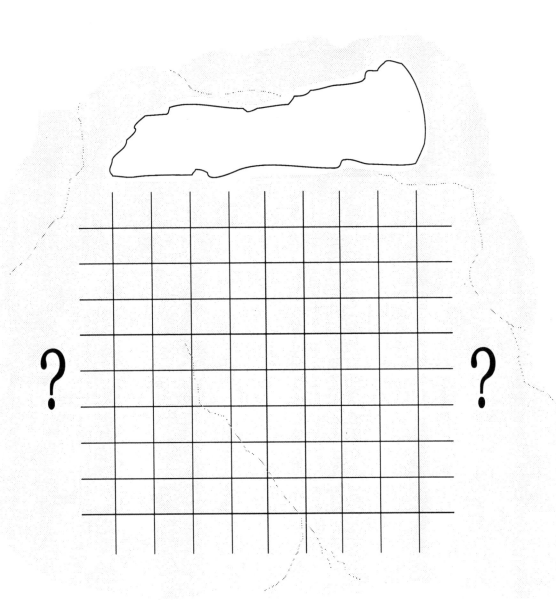

TRICKS FOR TRAINERS II

SECTION FIVE

Braintwisters

This section contains EIGHT different brainteasers.
When presented by the trainer in a challenging manner it
always makes an audience think creatively and sets the mood
for a great time of interaction.

WHAT IS THE LARGEST
AMERICAN COIN THAT CAN
BE PLACED ON THE
TABLETOP WITHOUT
TOUCHING ANY OF ITS
SIDES?

BRAINTWISTER #1

A picture of a table is placed on the overhead. What is the largest American coin that can be placed on the tabletop without touching any of its sides? The answer will surprise everyone!

Use the transparency master on the opposite page to make an overhead transparency. Ask the trainees to share their guesses.

They will be shocked to find that not even a penny can be placed on the table without touching the sides!!!

Our perspectives make this puzzle impossible to solve without experimentation. Many situations are like that. . . don't be afraid to risk an experiment!

BRAINTWISTER #2

A transparency with a picture of an old lady is placed on the overhead. By turning it upside down, the lady changes into a young girl. It's all a matter of perspective!

Make an overhead transparency from the picture on the opposite page.

When you put the transparency on the overhead one way it is most definitely an older woman.

When you put it on the overhead upside down, it is certainly a young girl.

Both pictures have exactly the same number of straight lines and curves but the perspective of the viewer makes all the difference!

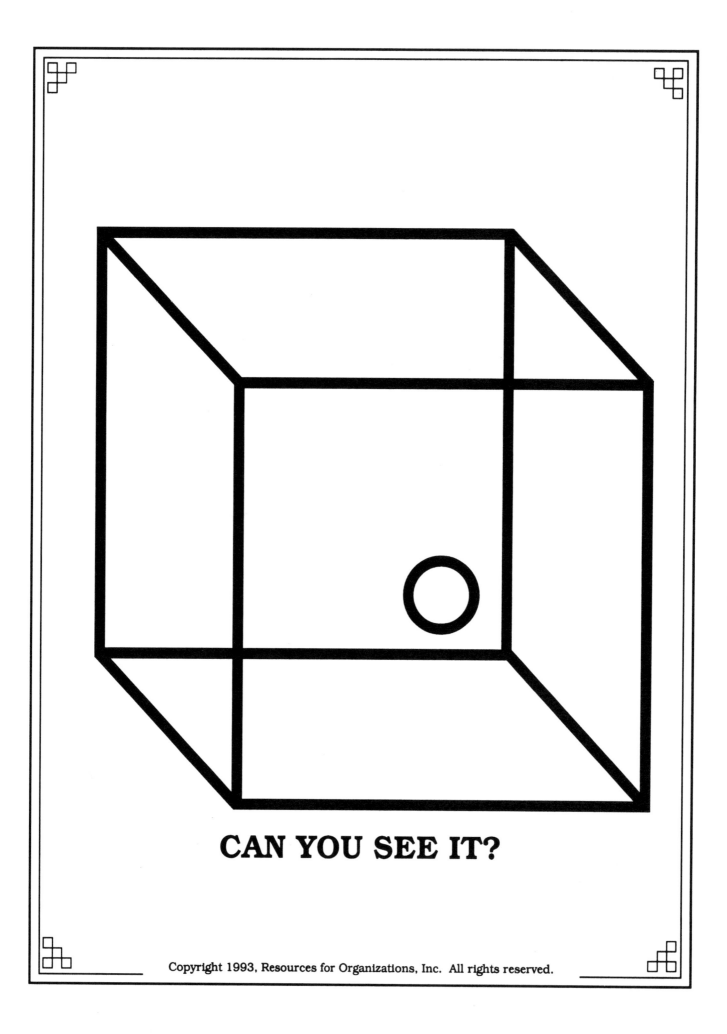

CAN YOU SEE IT?

BRAINTWISTER #3

Without moving this picture on the overhead, the class sees the picture from four different perspectives. The picture literally moves itself in their minds! A great illustration of differing viewpoints!

Make a transparency from the picture on the opposite page and place the transparency onto the overhead.

You don't need to touch or move the picture. It will all happen in the minds of the viewers.

Ask them if they can see the small circle. . .

1) at the lower right corner of the rear panel?

2) at the center of the front panel?

3) at the center of the back panel (with the cube lifted and angled to the left)?

4) at the lower right corner of the front panel?

After each question, give the group time to reorient their perspectives to see what you've just described.

What a great demonstration on the role of perspective in viewing the same situation from different perspectives.

Therein lies the heart of the creative process!

BRAINTWISTER #4

A picture of a Baker is on the overhead. Can anyone find the cow in the picture? As the picture is
turned upside down, the obvious picture of a
cow comes into view.

Make an overhead transparency from the picture.
Place the transparency on the overhead and then
turn the picture around slowly until the baker is
upside down.

Suddenly, a cow comes into view!

Again with the same number of straight lines and
curves, perspective shows its importance to what
we see in any situation!

This one is great to use in a series with
Braintwisters #2 & #3!

INSTRUCTIONS:

TAKE 1 GOLD BRICK
1" THICK AND USING
THE PATTERN CUT
THE BRICK EXACTLY
(8X8X1=64 CU. IN.)

REASSEMBLE THE
PARTS AS SHOWN
TO ADD ONE FREE
CUBIC INCH OF GOLD
(13X5X1=65 CU. IN.)

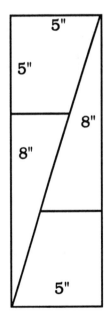

PATTERN FOR WEALTH!*

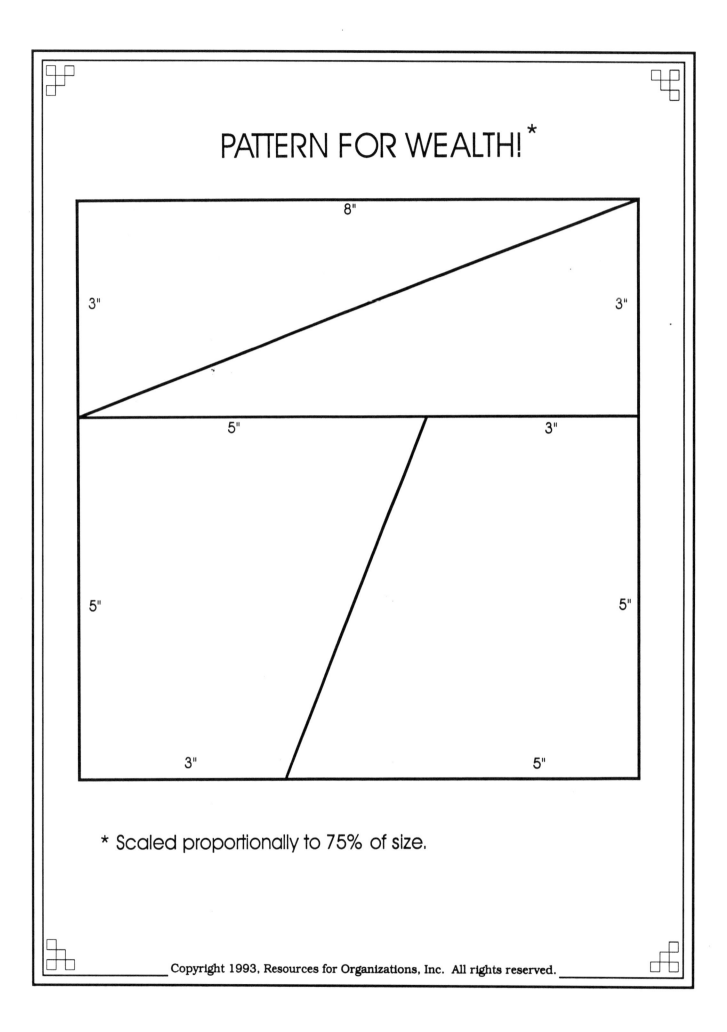

* Scaled proportionally to 75% of size.

BRAINTWISTER #5

A picture of a gold brick is cut into several pieces and reassembled only to find that it's grown one entire cubic inch! How can this work with the pieces remaining the same size!

Duplicate the opposite page so that each person in your training group gets a set. Give each person a pair of scissors and let them test it for themselves.

Have them figure the area (length x width) on the large picture before cutting the pieces apart. Then have them reassemble the pieces to match the smaller picture on that page. Have them figure the area again!

They will find that the area has now increased one square inch!

If this was a gold brick one inch thick, they would just have increased their gold supply by one cubic inch! Imagine the money they could make with this idea!

But why does it work?

This is great for helping a group understand that there certainly are some things they don't understand.

What an excellent attitude to have in the training room!

???????

HOW MANY TIMES WILL YOU NEED TO WRAP A STRING AROUND YOUR HEAD TO EQUAL YOUR HEIGHT?

???????

BRAINTWISTER #6

How many times will you need to wrap a string around your head in order to equal your height. The answer will surprise you, and you'll have fun proving it too!

Make a copy of the overhead transparency master on the opposite page and place it on your overhead. Have the class share their guesses.

Usually all are shocked when they actually experiment and find it only taking between two and three wraps of string around the head to equal the height.

Many things we cannot know very accurately without actual experimentation!

Tricks for Trainers II   **167**

BRAINTWISTER #7

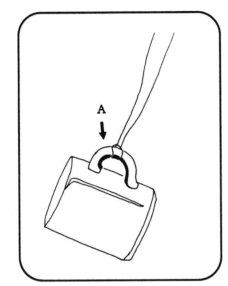

Can you remove the mug from the string hanging around your neck? It's not as easy as it sounds!

Cut a piece of string about three feet long and tie it into a circle.

Fold the string circle flat and insert one end through the handle of the mug. Then loop the other end through the string pulling it tightly against the mug handle.

Place the string around the neck of your volunteer so that the mug hangs freely. Can they remove the mug without removing the string from their neck? They will most likely attempt to unloop the string and move loop A up the string. However, they will find that the loop meets their neck and they can't undo the string.

When they attempt to take loop A around the cup, they will have found the solution!

Congratulate them and move onto the more challenging Braintwister #8!

BRAINTWISTER #8

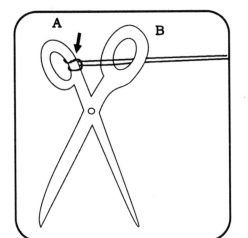

Can you remove the scissors from the string hanging around your neck? It's harder than the mug!

This great follow-up from the easier mug removal of Braintwister #7 also challenges the creative problem solving skills of the group!

Just as with the mug, loop the circle of string through one of the scissors handles as in the diagram.

However, as you can see from that diagram, run the string through the other handle before hanging it from the neck of your volunteer!

In order to remove the scissors, your volunteer will need to take the loop A as in the diagram along the double cord until it emerges from handle B. Then the loop can be passed over the entire scissors and removed!

Try it as a group project for even greater interaction among your trainees!

TRICKS FOR TRAINERS II

SECTION SIX

Bonus Section

This bonus section contains NINE quick ideas that add fun and excitement to training sessions by capitalizing on the unexpected!

PHONE NUMBER READING

At anytime during the training, convince the rest of the group that you can tell anyone their phone number without ever having met them!

The trainer walks up to one of the trainees and simply asks them to concentrate on their phone number! Taking out a small pad of paper, the trainer writes something on the pad as he attempts to ascertain the phone number by mental telepathy!

Suddenly, the trainer breathes a sigh of relief and asks the volunteer to join him in front of the group (he doesn't want to give the phone number out to everyone in the group).

The trainer asks the volunteer to tell the group what he wrote on the pad, and the volunteer replies that he did indeed write her phone number!

The class is impressed until the explanation is shared!

What the trainer actually writes on the pad is the phrase:

MY PHONE NUMBER

Later when he asks the volunteer to read what he wrote on the pad, the volunteer will indeed confirm to the group that he did indeed write "MY PHONE NUMBER!"

It's all perspective, assumptions, and communication!

PHONE BOOK THROW

When you toss this phone book to someone in the back row, everyone ducks! Then they laugh! Great fun! Things are not always what they first appear!

Prior to this demonstration take a city directory (as large as possible) and carefully remove the cover. Be careful not to tear it. Inside of this cover, cut and place a piece of thick foam (obtainable from most well-stocked fabric stores)—gluing the cover back onto the foam rubber.

Explain to the class that you have a little demonstration that uses a "foam book." Say these last two words without hesitation and nobody will question the fact that you said, "phone book."

Pick up your customized book and ask someone in the back of the room to please catch it. Without waiting for an answer, scale the book over the heads of the training class towards the person in the back.

People will duck and scream in reaction to a perceived danger! The analysis makes for great applications to communication, perception, and assumptions.

In other words, never judge a book by its cover!

THE SHIRT OFF MY BACK

Imagine grabbing someone's shirt by the collar and pulling it off even though they are still wearing their coat! You can!

What a great way to emphasize your commitment to your trainees! I know it's cliche but you would literally give them the shirt off your back! We need to be willing to do that for each other too!

With those words, walk up to someone in your training group and magically remove his shirt!

Your apparently spontaneous volunteer is really a secret accomplice that has been re-dressed for success!

In private, have him slip his arms out of his shirt sleeves—draping the sleeves over the top of his arms and buttoning them at his wrists. Have him unbutton all of buttons on his shirt with the exception of the top two. His tie will hide most of this. Then have him put his coat back on again.

It should look fairly ordinary.

As you get ready to conclude your presentation, invite him to the front of the training room and remove his tie to help him relax. Tell him that he still looks a little tense and have him unbutton his top few buttons and the buttons on his sleeve too. He should do his sleeves first and then he can hold his shirt closed with his hand. Now you're ready!

Dramatically grab his shirt by the collar and pull!

The shirt will be pulled free as his coat remains in place!

You will have closed your training session with a very visual and surprising portrayal of your commitment to the group and the group's commitment to each other!

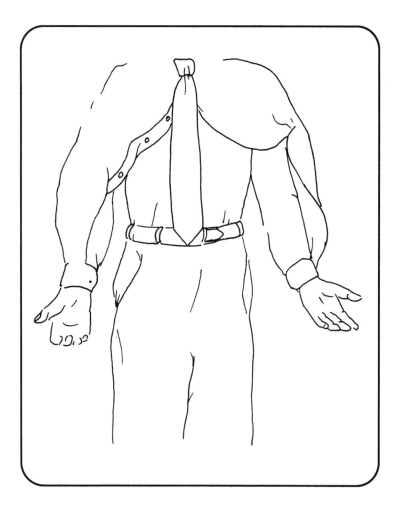

UNRAVELED

When one of your trainees is nice enough to pick at a thread on your coat, it suddenly pulls away and becomes over twenty feet in length!

Place a spool of contrasting thread inside your inner suitcoat pocket—using a needle to thread one end through your coat so that it lays on the outside of your jacket.

As soon as one of your more conscientious trainees reaches up to pick this loose thread off your coat, step back quickly and the person will appear to be unraveling your entire jacket!

Without reacting much, simply reach up and break the thread off throwing it away—thanking the person for helping you! Throw the thread away and go on with your training! The group will sit up straight not wanting to miss another moment of surprise from this most unusual trainer!

PRIZES! PRIZES! PRIZES!

These five prizes are perfect to use in a training situation! They sound so impressive. . . but are really so inexpensive!

Have fun with these prizes whenever you need to give out impressive sounding prizes (but you don't have any money in the budget)!

A BEAUTIFUL COPPER ENGRAVING OF OUR SIXTEENTH PRESIDENT turns out to be a penny!

A BRAND NEW WASHER AND DRYER turns out to be a paper towel and a regular circular washer from a hardware store.

A DIAMOND PIN turns out to be a "DIME AND PIN (safety pin)" each taken out of a beautiful jeweler's box.

A CRO-MAGNON WEATHER ROCK
Have a uniquely shaped rock to award—seriously announcing it as a recently discovered cro-magnon weather rock used by pre-historic cave dwellers. It is believed that the owner would set the rock outside on the ground and then use that rock to help him discern the weather using the following guidelines.

If the rock is wet . . . . it's RAINY.
If the rock is moving . . . . . . it's WINDY.

If the rock is cool . . . . it's COLD.
If the rock is hard to see . . . . it's FOGGY.
If the rock is casting a shadow. . it's SUNNY.

The most marvelous aspect of the rock is that it still
works today. . . millions of years later!

A BOX OF WATCHES?
You could also have a box on the front table from
which you remove several watches—describing the
merits of each one. Putting the watches back in the
box then play a game for "the whole box!" The group
will be very excited! At the conclusion of the game,
give away "the whole box." Yes. . . someone receives
the whole box—empty of course.

But they can't deny that they did receive "the whole box!"

A CADILLAC?
Finally, stop at a gas station and pick up an empty
windshield wiper blade box from their trash. When
you get ready to award this secret "mystery prize,"
phrase it like this

"YOU ARE THE PROUD WINNER OF A BRAND NEW
(PAUSE) CADILLAC (PAUSE) WINDSHIELD (PAUSE)
WIPER (PAUSE) BLADE (PAUSE) BOX!"

When those words are spoken with just the right
amount of pause between each component, the result
is hilarious. Award the empty wiper box with great
bravado!

A FINAL TRICK
WITH TRICKS 4 TRAINERS VOL II
USE THIS BOOK TO MAKE MAGIC!

Hand this copy of Tricks For Trainers Vol. II to a volunteer in your class.

Have the volunteer write down a three digit number. Now have them multiply their number by 9. Finally have them add the digits together in their new answer until they have only a single digit answer.

Finally have them divide this single digit number by 2—turning to the page in the book that corresponds to their final answer.

EXAMPLE:

Any three digit number 795
Multiply by 9...7155
Add the digits together...................................18
Add the digits together until you get
a singe digit answer 9
Divide by 2 ....4 ½
The answer will always be 4 ½!

Have them now turn to the page in the book that corresponds to their number—concentrating on ANY word on that page!

IMAGINE their surprise when they actually do find a page 4 ½ in this book! Imagine the look on their face when they find only one word on that page—a special one word message written by you to either open, close, or illustrate your training content!

DAVE ARCH

Author of all five books in the Tricks For
Trainers Resource Library (Tricks for
Trainers I & II, First Impressions, Lasting
Impressions, and The Idea Book), Dave Arch has
pioneered the use of magic in his motivational
programs and training.

Since 1982, magic has proven itself an
effective communication tool for groups as
diverse as hospital CEO's to sales representa-
tives to banking administrators.

Combining a ten year background in personal
and family counseling with a professional exper-
tise in magic, Dave travels from his home in
Omaha, Nebraska, to present his unique presentations before some 25,000 people each year in
both corporate and conference settings.

Whether he's using a power saw to saw an audience
volunteer in half or attempting to escape from a
regulation straitjacket, his audiences long remember both the excellent content and the entertaining
audience involvement that have become the trade-
marks of his successful presentations.

ROBERT W. PIKE, CSP

Robert has developed and implemented training programs for business, industry, government and the professions since 1969. As president of Resources For Organizations, Inc., Creative Training Techniques International, Inc., and The Resources Group Inc., Bob leads sessions over 150 days per year covering topics of leadership, attitudes, motivation, communication, decision-making, problem-solving, personal and organizational effectiveness, conflict management, team building and managerial productivity. More than 50,000 trainers have attended the Creative Training Techniques© workshop. As a consultant, Bob has worked with such organization as Pfizer, Upjohn, Caesars Boardwalk Regency, Exhibitor Magazine, Hallmark Cards Inc. and IBM.

Over the years, Bob has contributed to magazines like "Training," "The Personal Administrator" and "The Self Development Journal." He is editor of the "Creative Training Techniques Newsletter" and is author of "The Creative Training Techniques Handbook," "Developing, Marketing and Promoting Successful Seminars and Workshops" and "Improving Managerial Productivity."

THE TRICKS FOR TRAINERS RESOURCE LIBRARY

Tricks For Trainers, Vol I

Tricks For Trainers, Vol II

First Impressions/Lasting Impressions

Other Complementary Products/Services:
Trainer Bingo
The Magic Coloring Book

Seminars on these topics are also available by calling the Creative Training Techniques Companies.

The Creative Training Techniques Companies

Resources for Organizations, Inc.
Creative Training Techniques, Int'l, Inc.
The Resources Group, Inc.

The creation of these three companies has resulted in working together for one goal: to help clients achieve exceptional results with the application of innovative and creative training and development technologies.

Resources for Organizations, Inc. (ROI) was the first of the three companies which make up the successful Creative Training Techniques Companies. ROI is committed to

---

providing resource materials which enhance the results of your training.

The resources Bob Pike and his master trainers use during their seminars are available through the Resources for Organizations, Inc. (ROI) catalog. Many of ROI's products, like Tricks for Trainers, can turn training sessions into fun, stimulating, and memorable experiences. While other materials, which are rich in content, are full of practical and useful "how to" techniques. Whether it is integrating new interactive learning activities or utilizing training props, trainers at any level can enhance their sessions with these simple yet powerful tools.

In addition to this variety of training materials, activities, books, and props, ROI is the exclusive source for the audio cassette tape program featuring Bob Pike leading the popular two-day Creative Training Techniques© workshop.

Creative Training Techniques International, Inc. (CTTI) conducts seminars and in-house programs to build trainers competencies with instructor led, participant centered techniques. As a result of these programs, Bob and his trainers are able to unleash the learning potential of adults. Whatever your level of experience, by attending these seminars, you will increase audience involvement, improve the clarity and organization of your presentation and ultimately get better results.

The Resources Group, Inc. (TRGI) focuses the application of Creative Training Techniques programs and products which develop a company's most important asset—its people. TRGI develops and distributes products and programs that address the "human side of enterprise," often called soft skills.

All of TRGI's programs and products use the Creative Training Techniques' process of high energy and high involvement, with a focus on the application of knowledge and skills to achieve results.

Whether your need is for effective training products, practical and dynamic seminars, or useful pre-packaged programs, the Creative Training Techniques companies can assist you in achieving your training and organizational aspirations. Please call (612) 829-1954 for further information and literature.

Tricks for Trainers II   **191**